ABOUT THE AUTHOR

Cecil Jenkins was educated at Trinity College, the University of Dublin, from which he holds the degrees of B.A., M.A., and Ph.D., and at the École Normale Supérieure in Paris. He taught for some years at the École Normale Supérieure de Saint Cloud and at the Institut des Hautes Études d'Interprétariat de la Sorbonne, before returning to a university post in Great Britain. He is at present Reader in French in the School of European Studies at the University of Sussex, but will be spending the academic year 1972-73 as Visiting Associate Professor at the University of British Columbia. His publications in volume form include, in addition to a novel, a general study of François Mauriac, a critical edition of Mauriac's *Thérèse Desqueyroux,* and a critical edition of Malraux's own most famous novel *La Condition Humaine.* He is now working on certain problematic aspects of immediately contemporary French thought.

ANDRÉ MALRAUX

by

Cecil Jenkins

This is a general critical study of André Malraux: novelist, 'man of action', art philosopher, and for ten years until 1969 President de Gaulle's Minister for Cultural Affairs. While the almost legendary reputation of this spectacular but still rather baffling figure makes it necessary to bring out the essential continuity underlying his many-sided and apparently fluctuating career—and thereby to consider his works on art and his changing political commitment—the final emphasis is placed on his achievement as a major and 'mythmaking' imaginative writer. In this connection, particular stress is laid on the remarkable originality of the novels of the 1920's, as well as on the artistic and human merits of *L'Espoir*. If this critic tends to dismiss the 'legend' and to take a cool view both of the intellectual content of Malraux's later 'tragic humanism' and of certain aspects of his political career, it is not through lack of sympathy with an author whom he has met on a number of occasions and for whom he has considerable personal admiration. The intention is rather to situate Malraux in such a way as to serve the longer-term interests of his reputation as an important imaginative writer.

ERIES

ire

ty

h, Emeritus

guages

TWAYNE'S WORLD AUTHORS SERIES (TWAS)

The purpose of TWAS is to survey the major writers —novelists, dramatists, historians, poets, philosophers, and critics—of the nations of the world. Among the national literatures covered are those of Australia, Canada, China, Eastern Europe, France, Germany, Greece, India, Italy, Japan, Latin America, the Netherlands, New Zealand, Poland, Russia, Scandinavia, Spain, and the African nations, as well as Hebrew, Yiddish, and Latin Classical literatures. This survey is complemented by Twayne's United States Authors Series and English Authors Series.

The intent of each volume in these series is to present a critical-analytical study of the works of the writer; to include biographical and historical material that may be necessary for understanding, appreciation, and critical appraisal of the writer; and to present all material in clear, concise English—but not to vitiate the scholarly content of the work by doing so.

André Malraux

By CECIL JENKINS

The University of Sussex

Twayne Publishers, Inc. :: New York

Preface

While André Malraux is certainly one of the most spectacular figures among major writers alive today—and quite glitteringly successful, in that not only was he a "friend of genius" for the late President de Gaulle, but he has seen his writings presented in a selection for schools by the general's successor Georges Pompidou—he remains a controversial and faintly baffling one for the French public as for the Anglo-Saxon reader. One reason is the many-sided nature of a career which has combined fiction with adventure, archaeology, politics, publishing, and art philosophy. Another is the much-discussed switch to Gaullism after the last war of this novelist who, long before the term had been invented, had seemed the very exemplar of the left-wing "committed writer." Above all, there is the general blurring effect of the extraordinary legend surrounding Malraux's career as "man of action" in the East in the 1920s, in the Spanish Civil War, in the Resistance and, finally, as minister for cultural affairs during the first ten years of the Fifth Republic. In fact, Malraux still impinges as something of a myth which must be seen as a total phenomenon.

Although I am persuaded that in the end Malraux's importance is essentially that of the imaginative writer, I have therefore tried to make his overall career intelligible to the reader, to place it in its own intellectual and political setting, and to evaluate his achievement not only as novelist but as art philosopher and politician. To cover every aspect of his activity, obviously, has not gone without a degree of compression—in particular, I should have liked to deal more fully with stylistic features of the novels. However, I have at the outset stood the "legend of the man of action" firmly on its head in order to bring out the fundamental point that Malraux is much less the "committed writer" as generally understood than, as he himself implicitly recognizes, an obsessional or "dominated" writer. If I adopt a chronological approach thereafter, it is because the essential continuity under-

lying his apparently disparate and fluctuating activities is not to be seen superficially in intellectual terms—as a philosophical system it might be less than impressive—but as an organic, developing unity achieving itself afresh in concrete artistic form from book to book. In a word, I see the coherence and ultimate value of Malraux's overall enterprise as being those of the "myth-maker."

I should make it clear that this is a critical study. Not only do I give rather short shrift to the "legend," but I take a somewhat cool view of Malraux's later "tragic humanism" and of certain aspects of his postwar political activity. As against this, I attempt to bring out the extraordinary originality of his novels of the late 1920s, and also to emphasize the qualities of *L'Espoir*. I may perhaps add that I have a considerable private admiration for Malraux, whom I have met at different times over the past twenty years and whom I have always found not only impressive, but refreshingly honest, down to earth, and quite outstandingly generous in talking about his fellow writers. I would hope that any criticism advanced in this general study is itself a function of this sympathy, and of the desire to serve the larger interests of his reputation as an imaginative writer.

Contents

Chronology

1901 André Malraux born in Paris, November 3.

1919 Having left school without completing his *baccalauréat*, starts part-time work with the Paris bookseller and editor René-Louis Doyon.

1920 Starts working for the publisher Kra. First articles in the minor reviews *Action* and *La Connaissance*.

1921 *Lunes en papier.* Marries Clara Goldschmidt (the future writer Clara Malraux, from whom he will separate in the mid-1930s). Over next two years, travels extensively in Europe and in North Africa, cultivates his interest in anthropology and Eastern art, and speculates—disastrously in the end—on the Stock Exchange.

1923- Archaeological expedition to Cambodia with Clara and his
1924 friend Louis Chevasson. For removing statuary from the ruined Buddhist temple of Banteai-Srey, is condemned to three years' imprisonment (the sentence being reduced on appeal in Saigon to one year, and later annulled in Paris). Granted a stay of execution, returns home in November 1924.

1925 Returns to Saigon to act as co-editor of *L'Indochine*, until the suppression of the newspaper by the authorities. Is affiliated with Kuomintang through the Young Annam League and visits Hong Kong before returning to Paris.

1926 *La Tentation de l'Occident.*

1928 *Les Conquérants. Royaume farfelu.* Engaged as reader and editor by Gallimard, with particular responsibility for art books and for organizing exhibitions—his extensive travels over next few years to the Near East, India, Japan, and the United States are closely connected with this interest. His association with Gallimard also brings him into close contact with Gide and other established writers.

1930 *La Voie royale.*

1931 Visits Shanghai, setting for *La Condition humaine.*

1933 *La Condition humaine.* Prix Goncourt.

1934 After a one-day flight over the Yemen desert in search of the legendary capital of the Queen of Sheba, attends Soviet Writers' Congress in Moscow, is active in such bodies as the Association des Écrivains et Artistes Révolutionnaires, and will emerge over next few years as one of France's leading anti-fascist writers.

1935 *Le Temps du mépris.*

1936 Goes to Spain at the start of the Civil War, forms on behalf of the Republicans an international air squadron, the "Escadre España," and flies on sixty-five missions in the early fighting as an air gunner.

1937 *L'Espoir.* Tours the United States and Canada on fund-raising trip for Spanish Republican cause.

1938 Makes film of *L'Espoir* in Spain.

1940 Captured with his tank unit during the fall of France, he escapes and makes his way into the "Zone Libre."

1943 *Les Noyers de l'Altenburg* (published in Switzerland).

1944- Active as Resistance leader, under the name of "Colonel
1945 Berger" (after the hero of *Les Noyers de l'Altenburg,* Vincent Berger), in the Dordogne. Wounded and taken prisoner by the Germans, is released by the liberating French forces, after which he distinguishes himself as commander of the volunteer Alsace-Lorraine Brigade in Alsace.

1945- Minister for information in de Gaulle's short-lived Provisional
1946 Government.

1947 Becomes director of propaganda and a leading spokesman for de Gaulle's newly founded Rassemblement du Peuple Français—active in this capacity until 1952. Is accused of "betraying the Left."

1951 *Les Voix du silence.*

1954 Expresses some sympathy with Mendès-France and the "New Left" in the weekly *L'Express.* Thierry Maulnier's stage adaptation of *La Condition humaine* presented at Théâtre Hébertot.

1957 *La Métamorphose des dieux.*

1958 Returns to power as minister attached to de Gaulle after Algiers *putsch.* Condemns torture in Algeria and offers to send as investigating committee the three Nobel Prize-winners Mauriac, Camus, and Martin du Gard.

1959 Appointed minister for cultural affairs, in which capacity he will visit many countries throughout the world over the next ten years. Begins reorganization of the National Theaters, restoration of public monuments in Paris and elsewhere, setting up of "Maisons de la Culture" in various towns, and other ministerial tasks.

1962 Unsuccessful attempt on his life by elements of the Right Wing extremist Organisation de l'Armée Secrète ("O.A.S."), opposed to de Gaulle's switch of policy over Algeria.

Chronology

CHAPTER 1

The Writer and the Myth

D ID Malraux, exasperated by de Gaulle's indecision over
seizing power in the late 1940s, *really* say: "Here we are
at last on the bank of the Rubicon, and what do *you* do? You
sit and fish!" "No" he says with a smile, "but it does sound very
like Malraux!" Does he speak the fifteen or seventeen languages
mentioned by certain biographical dictionaries? No: "only some
slight acquaintance with the dead languages, a little Chinese
and a few words of English." Does his handwriting, as one
lengthy journalistic account would have it, look "curiously like
hieroglyphic incisions in stone"? Curiously or not curiously, it
does not in the very least look like hieroglyphic incisions in
stone. And this is only to scratch the surface of the mass of
colorful apocrypha surrounding this writer whose fame as a
novelist of adventure and revolution has tended to be fused—
and confused—with the prestige of heroic action and of significant moments of history itself. Malraux, even today, impinges
primarily as a legend.

In order to see him at all clearly—and, indeed, to bring out
the value of his artistic enterprise—we must try at the outset
to deliver the writer from the myth.

I The Legend of the Man of Action

The reasons for the Malraux legend—which crystallized in the
mid-1920's with the fuss in the Paris newspapers following
upon his arrest in Indo China for removing valuable sculpture
from an abandoned temple—are obvious enough. To rise from
this youthful escapade, through antigovernment agitation in
the Far East and a rather glorious fighting role in both the
Spanish Civil War and the Resistance, to become the intimate
of the late President de Gaulle and his minister for cultural
affairs until they left power together in 1969: this has indeed

been a spectacular career. To have combined it with an immensely successful and apparently entirely parallel career as a
writer is, in this century, to border on the unique. Again, Malraux is an extraordinarily intense and compelling personality,
and above all a brilliant and voluble talker. Already in the
1920s, André Gide found it hard to keep up with him, while
Maurice Sachs described him as "a mixture of the young officer,
the dilettante and the Romantic poet; he talks very well, very
fast, appears to know absolutely everything, dazzles unfailingly,
and leaves you with the impression of having met 'the most
intelligent man of the century.'"[1]

In addition, the legend doubtless answered a need of the
times. For a whole generation of young intellectuals, as the rise
of fascism darkened the European situation in the 1930s, Malraux was one of those who provided the guarantee that the
man of letters was not necessarily a self-regarding figure in
carpet slippers in a carefully insulated study; he was seen as
the intellectual-in-action, as a Witness. Finally, of course, the
legend answered a need in Malraux himself and grew to the
extent that, to say the least, he never went out of his way to hold
it in check. In a transposed retrospective of his own career in
Les Noyers de l'Altenburg, he recognizes this clearly: "He might
perhaps have contrived to destroy the mythical figure he was
growing into, if he had tried. But he had no desire to do so.
His legend flattered him. More than that: he loved it."

Now I find it as pointless to indulge in sly innuendo about
the Malraux legend as to pretend that it does not constitute a
problem; it is simpler to be frank about it, but to try to understand. Legends are decorative and mainly harmless things, while
we should also remember that the lives of major writers are
open to more public scrutiny than would be welcomed by every
critic. Again, it might be unreasonable to expect the relationship
with reality of a highly original novelist to be that of the man
in the street; the very quality of Malraux's work derives from
a certain imperialism of the imagination, from a *confrontation*
with reality of great poetic intensity. Nevertheless this rather
garish legend, with which Malraux did not in fact begin to
coincide morally until the mid-1930s—by which time of course,
and ironically, he had begun to outgrow the need for it—has
become something of a nuisance, not least to Malraux himself.

There has long been a satirical "antilegend" in left-wing newspapers from the Communist *L'Humanité* to *Le Canard Enchaîné*.
In addition, Malraux's first wife, Clara Malraux—though I do
not think that she is to be blamed for this—has in several novels
and in recently published autobiographical volumes documented
his early "mythomania," or propensity for telling tall stories
about his own activities, at rather painful length.[2] In so far as
it is easy to point to the serious inflation of his revolutionary role
in the East in the 1920s, for example, the legend has rebounded
damagingly to obscure the true courage of this gifted and in
many ways admirable man, which has consisted as much in
confronting himself and his own "demons" through art as in
confronting the world in "action."

More generally, the legend has tended to obscure the continuity of Malraux's writing career. There is, for a start, the
apparent opposition between the novelist and the art-philosopher.
In fact, of course, Malraux did not "turn to art" late in life. His
first intellectual preoccupations were art, ethnology, and archaeology; he was engaged by Gallimard in the late 1920s largely
to edit art books and to organize exhibitions; he was working
toward his major writings in this field from the 1930s onward.
Indeed he suggests in conversation that he may perhaps be a
painter who missed his vocation, and says that for him: "*Les Voix
du silence* and *La Condition humaine* are one and the same
thing." If he chose art as the field of demonstration of a philosophical or even a political argument, it was to a large extent
because this is the area with which he is most familiar.

The other major "mystery" of Malraux's career, that of the
revolutionary turned Gaullist, is rather more complex. His own
view of this *volte face*: that it is not he who changed, but rather
the world and in particular the Communists, is clearly not entirely satisfactory—since he continued to live in a dynamic
relationship with this world and since the causes he has espoused
are far from being politically or morally identical. Nevertheless, as his own thought emerges, and as the element of philosophical opportunism or higher tactics in his affiliation with
these causes becomes evident, it will be seen that what is
striking about Malraux's career is less its external fluctuation
than its fundamental underlying continuity. The pessimism of
the Malraux of the Cold War period—the idea that "Man is

dead," or the skepticism expressed in *Les Voix du silence* with regard to "progress, science, reason, and democracy"—is essentially that of the young essayist of *La Tentation de l'Occident* and "D'une jeunesse européenne." Indeed, if a hostile critic wished seriously to probe this aspect of Malraux, he would do better to observe what is *really* surprising about this fluctuating Man of Action: that the whole body of work up to the present should depend far less upon the lessons of action than upon a set of stark concepts developed by the author in his early twenties, almost fifty years ago.

The main reason why the legend has become a nuisance, however, is that it has surrounded Malraux's work with a set of false assumptions to the extent of blurring the nature of his activity as a writer. It suggests a man dedicated to historical action, whereas Malraux's activity before 1958 was highly selective and intermittent: like the hero of *Les Conquérants* he was less a man of action than "a man capable of action—on occasion." It suggests ideological commitment, whereas Malraux's political options have been essentially pragmatic, and usually negative rather than positive. In the Far East in the 1920s he was something of an adventurer; in Europe in the mid-1930s he was an anti-fascist. He was never philosophically a Marxist, and never a Communist. One ironic result of the misunderstanding has been that *L'Espoir*, which he himself regards as his greatest achievement—and which contains more explicit criticism of the Communists than any of his other novels—was until recently often written off as party propaganda.

Above all, of course, the legend suggests the on-the-spot reporter or journalistic novelist tied to realism, and a number of French critics who should know better have tended, by the use of vague and noble terms such as "absolute witness," to maintain this confusion. However, the sort of special authority which the legend conferred upon *La Condition humaine*, for example, was at odds not merely with the facts but with the artistic force and the moral meaning of the novel. It was widely seen as an eyewitness account of Chiang Kai-shek's dramatic break with the Communists in 1927 by a participant who had directed the Kuomintang's nationalist propaganda in the key southern provinces over the previous two years. Now Malraux, though active earlier in Indo China, did no more than spend a few days in

Hong Kong before returning to France around the end of 1925, a good fifteen months before the events in question, and it was only years afterwards that he set foot in China proper.

Similarly, *Les Conquérants* and *La Voie royale* are not so much "reports" on what Malraux did in the East as, more precisely, since he is an inventive rather than a documentary novelist, stylized treatments of what he did *not* do in the East. In fact the only one of Malraux's six novels which depends at all fully or directly upon his own immediate action is *L'Espoir,* written during the Spanish Civil War, and even here the events are firmly subordinated by this deliberate artist to the recurring themes of the whole of his work. What the legend tends to obscure, absurdly enough, is that Malraux is a major imaginative writer.

That Malraux's has been a spectacular career is obvious. That there has been a certain running continuity between his "action" and his writing is also clear. Nevertheless, in order to enter into the world of this writer—and an anguished and solitary world it is—one has to take this golden legend of the Man of Action and stand it firmly on its head. For Malraux is not in the ordinary meaning of the term a "committed writer" at all. Indeed he sees himself by implication as being in some sense the opposite: a "dominated writer."

II *The "Dominated Writer"*

Malraux has been not so much the privileged spokesman of the real world as the tormented visionary looking beyond the present struggles of men to the permanent tragedy of "Man": not so much the novelist of history, in fact, as the poet of what he everywhere calls "destiny."

This key term is not actually employed by him with any great rigor—he sometimes uses it in a merely rhetorical or popular sense. In general, however, and in a way which strikingly anticipates the existentialist positions of Sartre and Camus, he uses it to denote all those factors governing human existence—time, suffering, death, the arbitrariness of birth and of situation, the ultimate solitude of the individual—which tend to deny man and to make his presence in an indifferent and contingent universe seem "absurd." Basically, therefore, it refers

to those elements *permanently* constituting the "human condition." Nevertheless, he also sees the idea of destiny as pecu-
liarly appropriate to our own time and indeed, to quote *Les Voix
du silence*, as the "Spectre of the 20th Century." For Malraux—
as will emerge more fully in the next chapter—does not simply
believe with the German philosopher Nietzsche of the end of
last century that "God is dead." He feels that our idea of man
has collapsed as a result, and that human life will seem intoler-
able unless our agnostic culture can somehow contrive to give
the individual a "soul" and relate him to the universe as fully
as did the great religions.

"The modern world," he wrote in 1927, "carries within itself,
like a cancer, its lack of a soul. It will not free itself from this
absence, implied by its own law. And it will continue thus until
men are convulsed by a collective call to the soul."[3] "The next
century's task," he told an interviewer from *Time* in 1955, "will
be to rediscover its gods."[4] In fact for most of his career, Malraux, pessimistic as he is about human reason and the other
values of the agnostic humanism now largely dominating our
culture, has tended to treat our time as a kind of dark, unreal,
and violent interlude between Christianity and the next universal religion. Which is some indication of the Romantic remove
at which fundamentally this "helmeted angel," as Chavardès
calls him, has stood in relation to the philosophical values normally associated with revolutionary action.[5]

Now, at one level, Malraux's aesthetic of the novel corresponds
entirely to this stark perspective. Like Greek tragedy which, as
he constantly argues, was a "questioning of man's destiny"—and
an "antidestiny" in that the very representing of fate constitutes
a moral victory over fate—the novel of our "age of interrogation"
is properly the tragic poem of Man and his Destiny. This already
devalues the story of men in their history of course, as it also
devalues psychological analysis, which Malraux sees as expressive of a bankrupt individualism, and largely pointless in a
civilization which has no clear idea of man.

"The modern novel," he writes, "is in my view a privileged
means of expressing the tragedy of man, and not an elucidation
of the individual."[6] The emphasis therefore moves away from
the social novel or the character novel, implying a belief in the
opaque reality of the human world, toward the novel of situa-

tion—"I don't start with the characters," Malraux insists in conversation, "I start from the situation." However, it is not easy to
translate the elliptical idea of destiny into the terms of the
relative world, the more so since the developed life of society
tends to conceal the "human condition." Inevitably, therefore,
we move toward the *extreme* situation—self-assertion against the
jungle, revolution, war—which not only makes possible but also
confers the necessary historical status upon the supreme moment
in which the human act, affirming itself against the world, can
assume its full metaphysical significance.

There is obviously something of a vicious circle about all this,
in that Malraux's essentially antihistorical vision tends ironically
to depend for its force upon the force of history itself. It is
significant that in the three novels which he privately regards
as unsuccessful—*La Voie royale, Le Temps du mépris,* and *Les
Noyers de l'Altenburg*—he was operating without the pressure
and the prestige of the revolutionary situation. Even so, he
everywhere bends the novel of history to the poem of destiny.

Plot and external conflict, expressive of the world's continuity,
are as far as possible subordinated to what for him is the real
conflict: between the character and life itself, between his
will to metaphysical meaning and his finitude. The "scenes"
tend to be separate "vertical" moments of time or intensity juxta-
posed as by a cinematic editing technique. The narrative method
tends to subordinate external reality to the consciousness of
the character viewing it. The temporal is seen in the light
of the eternal. In fact, the Malraux hero—like the writer himself
—is not so much the integrated "man of action" as, in Emmanuel
Mounier's excellent coinage, the "metapractician" living out tragically in historical action that denial of merely historical definition
which is his "destiny."[7] And of course it is this very ambiguity,
this constant tension between the optimistic ethos of collective
action and his own dark pessimism with regard to the metaphysical situation of the individual, which gives Malraux's novels
their force and their distinctive flavor.

So far, however, we have dealt only with the external side
of Malraux's aesthetic, and it would be foolish—working backward from his recently formulated "tragic humanism"—to see
him as using the novel in order to illustrate a clearly defined
philosophical view of "destiny" and of "Man." This would be

to fail to appreciate the inner necessity which gives his work
its compulsion and, in effect, to put his career as a writer back
to front. For one thing, his first three novels in particular are
not at all coherent at the level of ideas; his control here is
organic, that is to say: *artistic*. For another, his aesthetic—which
he began to formulate implicitly in various reviews and minor
writings in the early 1930s—was a rationalization of his existing
practice, and he was in fact driven beyond it by the reality
of the historical world toward epic, in *L'Espoir*.

Above all, it is patent that the force of Malraux's novels does
not spring from the intellectual manipulation of symbolical
elements relating to "Man." It springs rather, as the unconscious
repetition of minor detail everywhere indicates, from the *obsessional* consistency of this fictional world of male intellectuals
haunted by solitude and separateness, with its basic trauma of
venture and defeat, its central claustrophobic scenes, its fears of
blindness and madness and loss of identity, its temptations to
pain and violence and glory and godhead. It is a commonplace of
Malraux criticism to suggest that his characters are generally
recognizable as a series of different projections of himself. "Man,"
in other words, and inevitably enough, is the abstract of André
Malraux himself and indeed, one might almost say, the central
Malraux myth.

In effect, of course, Malraux has recognized this. He has long
insisted that the true writer is not one who represents but one
who invents, not one who renders the world but one who—by
using the world as raw material, as a backcloth or plausible surface for the private fiction—creates a coherent and compelling
world of his own. Even self-conscious "realism" in his view,
and I think rightly, is less the rendering of reality than the *rectification* of reality to meet the needs of the imperializing private
vision. The significant novelist, for him, is not one who offers
"reality," but one who reorders reality in accordance with a
powerful and coherent myth. And it is precisely the consistency
of this private or "autonomous" world which provides the "density," the "tone," and the "mystery" which he looks for as signs of
quality in the work of his fellow writers.

Here again, of course, it emerges that it is pointless to look
in Malraux's own novels for a straightforward account of historical events—and quite irrelevant to see them as being *romans*

à clef. To take the single case of *La Condition humaine* as an
example, there may well be something of the historical André
Berthelot about the character Ferral, of the journalist René
Guetta about the engaging Clappique, of André Gide's appearance and manner, and of Bernard Groethuysen's role of *maître
à penser* about the wise old Gisors, and of the Japanese writer
Kyoshi Komatsu about his son Kyo (a short form for Kyoshi).
Indeed it is clear that May is based on Clara Malraux herself—
and since the only other developed woman character in the
novels, Valérie of this same work, was doubtless suggested less
by life than by Laclos's *Les Liaisons dangereuses* which much
interested Malraux at this time, the fact is not without significance. Even so, these originals were in their varying ways merely
supports for thematic possibilities dictated by the situation,
and they are transmuted until their reality as fictional characters is essentially a function of the parts they play within the
highly distinctive "autonomous" world of the novel. Ferral, Clappique, Gisors, and Kyo are as it were standard roles in the
running moral debate between the various self-projections of
Malraux himself.

To return to Malraux's own aesthetic, however, what then is
it which drives the novelist to try to tame the world, to exorcise
it magically by possessing it through myth? By implication he
classes himself with such novelists as Dostoevsky and Faulkner
as a "dominated writer," by which he means one driven to
resolve a private obsession through projection. The "dominated
writer" involves the world in his obsession in order to objec-
tivize and justify the obsessional vision, and in the end, perhaps,
to dissipate the obsession and feel at one with other men. Even
if the writer is in a sense making a compromise with reality
on his own terms, the imaginative enterprise is the overcoming
of a form of solitude, the conquest of what separated the artist
from others or from the world.

It will already be apparent that, at least in regard to the novel,
Malraux does not reject out of hand a very broad type of "Freudian" explanation, though with the very important reservation
that no such explanation can account for what really matters, the
quality of the work—he says with rather grim jocularity in conversation: "there is also the little problem that we call talent."
At all events, in a speech of 1934 entitled "L'Attitude de l'artiste,"

he declares: "it is no longer a question of depicting a world, as was said of Balzac, but of expressing through a set of images the development of a personal problem."[8] And a year later, in his review of Gide's *Les Nouvelles Nourritures,* he speaks in general terms of the world as being for the writer merely the "means of expression, more or less vast, of a private drama."

Now while I am as far as possible respecting Malraux's private life, even in the Chronology, the legend itself imposes some consideration of the sort of man that he is. This is the more the case in that, all too predictably, speculation about his own "private drama"—ranging happily from epilepsy or drug addiction to Claude Mauriac's dark suggestion that the similarity of scenes of killing in the novels implies a "precise memory, a constant and immutable reference" haunting the author[9]—has tended to become part and parcel of the vicious circle of the legend itself. The truth, I am persuaded, is a great deal less exotic than these tales. However, it is worth glancing at this aspect, since it leads us fairly quickly to the "essential" Malraux underlying his apparently disparate manifestations as adventurer, novelist, art-philosopher, and politician. This Malraux, and I am not using the term pejoratively, is the myth-maker.

III   *The Myth-maker*

In 1937, when on a fund-raising visit to the United States, Malraux told some Hollywood journalists that he was fighting in Spain because, as he put it, he did not like his life. In fact, there was perhaps a trace of coquetry in this remark. It is true that the early Malraux hero had also "disliked his life," and that the novels up to this point are marked by a deep sense of estrangement—which many of those who knew him discerned in the writer himself. Even so, the descriptions of him at the time of the Spanish Civil War, and the new relaxed tone of *L'Espoir* itself, suggest a considerable change in the man at this period. Gaëtan Picon, at one time almost the official Malraux critic, has suggested that he is obsessed with the idea of "virile fraternity" to the very extent that it escapes him.[10] My own impression is that the immediately "haunting" nature of Malraux's sense of estrangement was to a great extent dissipated— paradoxically enough in the climate of war—by his first real experience of comradeship with other men in Spain, when the legend at last came true, and then in the Resistance. It was probably this factor which removed the compulsion to express himself through fiction and left him free, after the war, to pursue his writer's "obsession" in secondary, intellectualized terms in his art writings and political speeches. Certainly, if one grants a certain nervous and intellectual intensity, he has in recent years shown himself both warm and at ease in private.

Nevertheless the remark quoted is indicative, and it should serve to warn us against too rapid or total a denunciation of Malraux's "mythomania." While I agree with Denis Boak, for example, that Malraux must be held responsible for many of the early stories surrounding him, I find his suggested picture of a man coldly setting about "the deliberate creation of legend late in the 1920s" with the use of "modern publicity methods"[11] inherently implausible at the simple psychological level. If a man were as much in control of himself as this suggests, he could probably have done without the legend—*and* the novel-writing, of course—in the first place. But, in fact, Malraux had been a compulsive myth-maker since his adolescence, and naïve enough to let this compulsion run him into heavy humiliation after his arrest in Indo China. If a man as intelligent as Malraux shortsightedly misrepresents easily verifiable facts, it is fairly clearly because at this time his *need* for a legend went hand in hand with a certain innocence about the world. The emphasis might better be placed, not on the haughtiness, but on the essential *vulnerability* which it and the legend served to protect—a vulnerability which was perhaps not totally appreciated by Clara Malraux herself.

That she should, in two novels and now in the successive volumes of her autobiography: *Le Bruit de nos pas*, in effect be saying the same thing over and over again is amply indicative of the indelibly painful experience of living with a young man whom she much admired, but who appeared to deny her existence by excluding her publicly and privately from an elected legend in which he alone must play the leading part. And a book like *Nos Vingt ans* achieves general interest as a picture of the strained beginnings of equality between the sexes in the France of the 1920s. Again, she saw sympathetically that his myth-making—significantly, to begin with, about his

family background—was a form of over-compensation for an
unhappy childhood in the course of which, after the separation
of his parents, he and his mother lived for a time with his
grandmother, who ran a small grocery store at Bondy, just
outside Paris.

However, she hardly discerned the depth of the pain underlying what she now calls his "misogyny," and which was apparently due largely to the classically ambivalent feelings of a
proud and self-assertive boy, and only child, toward the abandoned mother in the situation of a broken marriage. Although her
feminist case has a certain general validity, there was much
naïveté in her own attitude to the episode of her infidelity, later
transposed as that of May in *La Condition humaine*; already
surprised that he himself had been faithful, she seems to have
been taken aback by the extent of his distress when she insisted
on recounting this incident. What she appears not to have realized, ironically enough, was the extent of his admiration for
and dependence upon herself. At all events, her books cannot
simply be taken as providing convenient ammunition with which
to attack her former husband.

What is interesting about all this is not so much the details
of a crisis of adolescence which, given this family situation, is
after all of a fairly standard kind, but rather Malraux's own
attitude to it. In an interview with Jean Farran in 1954 he
says bitterly: "the family milieu had no importance for me; it
was unreal."[12] But of course it *was* real, and *decisively* important—and hardly to be "obliterated from his memory," as Farran
suggests. Indeed, the measure of the humiliation it imposed is
not so much that he should invent a more satisfying personal
history—that again is a standard reaction, and one that can be
superseded—nor even that he should deny the reality of his own
history. It is rather his tendency to deny the very principle
underlying the reality.

This is well illustrated, as it happens, by his very obvious
alter ego, Roger, in Clara Malraux's early novel *Portrait de
Grisélidis*, who inveighs against all the conditioning factors
operating upon men and declares: "in fact, I should not be
surprised to learn one day that we inherit nothing from our
forebears but material goods, and that each of us starts life as
if he were the first, the unique...."[13] For Malraux begins—and

ends, one might almost say—with an instinctive rejection of the facts of his own background and, by extension, of the controlling factors of heredity, history, and environment inevitably governing the life of the individual. The intellectual influences operating upon him did not cause this rejection; they merely fed it, and justified it.

This drive to deny normally accepted reality becomes the principle which—at every level, and with an almost hallucinatory consistency—governs Malraux's world and everywhere turns him into the myth-maker.

It dictates the rejection of the immediate reality of life in favor of the myth of "destiny"; the aesthetic of the novel which places value not on the rendering of "reality" but upon the coherence of the myth; the antirationalist bias against science, psychology, political doctrine, and intellectual *system* in general. It dictates the concomitant need that truth, if it cannot reside in system, should be incarnated in great men, and that they should not appear to be reducible to any conditioning explanation—de Gaulle, he told Farran, was beyond the interpretations of psychology.[14] It dictates the need in *Les Voix du silence* to deliver the artist, seen as the highest expression of Man, from every kind of historical, social or psychological determinism— even at the cost of separating him from his historical self. It dictates the great rhetorical questions as to whether Man is dead, whether democracy is dead, whether Europe is dead. It leads with smooth inevitability toward the title of the final memoirs: *Antimémoires*.

It underlies the legend itself, of course. For to deny one's own reality is to deprive the world itself of reality. Whence the equivalence of truth and myth for the young Malraux, the sense that life consisted in playing or gambling with a set of optional "realities" or possibilities, and the initial attitude—well expressed by "Roger" in *Portrait de Grisélidis*"—that "the idea that an action should commit or limit us has always seemed to me to be mad."[15] But it also underlies the anguish bordering on panic which characterizes Malraux's fictional world up to the mid-1930s. For playing with life can be a grim gamble indeed. To deny one's own reality, and thereby divest the world of reality, is to sacrifice the continuity of past into present and leave oneself disarmed in the face of an unpredictable future: to create

a vacuum haunted by the fear of death or madness or anything
that threatens the simple sense of being alive which is the only
remaining term of identity. Whereupon, it begins to underlie
the need to find in the extreme situation the sense of self and
of fraternity which cannot be achieved at the ordinary level
of living; the need to borrow a little meaning from the historical
world, whether it be "real" or not; and the continuing need of
this absolutist who cannot intellectually return to the religion
which he learned at his mother's knee to find for an agnostic
humanist culture some equivalent of the Christian soul: some
essence untainted by the relativity of the world which might
enable him to realize his myth of "fundamental Man."

The real adventure of this spectacular latter-day Romantic,
therefore, has been a strangely intense confrontation with
reality over half a century which makes the "legend" itself
look like the subromantic tinsel which, amusing or not, it very
largely is. It is a kind of onslaught on the impossible: the story
of a man who self-protectively *elects* the estrangement originally
imposed upon him but who is nevertheless driven, from within
this haunted antiworld of his own making, to look for values
or at least viable myths. Inevitably enough, it in some ways
constitutes a cautionary tale. However, the energy and the talent
of this man make it a dramatic one. The fact that it is conducted
in relation to some of the most poignant moments of twentieth-
century history makes it a challenging one. And, finally, there
is about this estranged myth-maker a certain aristocratic nobility
and a constant *will* to humanity which make it a moving one.

CHAPTER 2

The "Young European"

I   Crisis of the Mind

"BETWEEN eighteen and twenty, life is like a stock exchange where you buy shares not with money but with
acts," said Malraux to the Franco-American writer Julien Green
over lunch one day in 1930. "Most men buy nothing at all."[1]

The year in which Malraux reached eighteen was 1919: the
year of the Treaty of Versailles, of the rejoicing after the storm
which was to lead into the "aspirin age" of the Gay Twenties.
There was talk of the League of Nations, of universal peace.
France still seemed a great power, and Paris the intellectual and
artistic capital of the world. The café life of the artists, shifting
gradually from Montmartre to Montparnasse, was gay. And the
writers themselves got caught up in this new and hectic world
of aeroplanes, motor cars, radio, cinema, jazz, world travel,
and sport. Einstein inadvertently provided the popular mind
with a label for this exciting and mobile world. Space, time,
social conventions, moral values: everything seemed suddenly
to be "relative." And relative in more ways than one. . . .

For the Treaty of Versailles had created as many problems
as it had solved, and it was already apparent to some that not
only France, but Europe itself had lost its place. The two great
powers were no longer France and Great Britain, but the United
States and the new Soviet Russia. Communism was then sweeping
into Germany and Hungary—the year 1919 marks the birth of the
Third International. And it is also the year of Paul Valéry's
famous essay "La Crise de l'esprit," beginning: "We civilizations know now that we are mortal," in which he stated the
profound moral shock to thinking people that the war had
caused.[2] How could a civilization based on reason, progress,
and science have led to this? How could everyday virtues of

27

effort and discipline have been put to such ends? Was not European culture, if only because of its composite relativism— "its three hundred different ways of explaining the world, its thousand and one different shades of Christianity, its dozens of positivisms"—a "lost illusion"? It is with the growth of this disquiet that the more static pre-1914 period came gradually to look like the *Belle Époque.*

In fact, of course, many of the new influences combining to undermine rationalism, the integrity of the personality and existing values—Dostoevsky, Nietzsche, Freud, Bergson, Pirandello, Gide, Proust—were prewar forces only now coming into their own as the blind revolt of the new generation began. With the "enterprise of demolition" that was Dada, and then with the more organized Surrealism, the instability of the world was shortly elevated almost into a system. Reason gave way to the unconscious, reality to a new poetic suprareal, and all that represented the established order—patriotism, religion, and traditional moral attitudes—was denounced as a new "psychic revolution" got under way. However, there was youthful exuberance as well as despair behind the "scandalous" manifestations of these young writers, and it would seem that the tall, thin and rather elegant young man who turned up at René-Louis Doyon's bookshop one day in 1919 responded similarly to both the exciting and the disquieting aspects of the time.

He astonished Doyon with his expertise, and proceeded to supplement his income from his father and grandmother by supplying the bookseller systematically with rare editions picked up for a song at the stalls along the quays. He also became involved in Doyon's modest publishing ventures and new review *La Connaissance,* before starting in 1920 to write for the review *Action* and to edit texts for the minor publisher Simon Kra. He edited or re-edited some Symbolist pieces before embarking on an up-to-date series, including volumes by Max Jacob and Pierre Reverdy. At dinners organized by *Action,* and in connection with the illustrations for these editions, he came across painters as well as writers; he met Galanis, Fernand Léger, Juan Gris, and Picasso. By 1922, even if Jacques Rivière found him intellectually rather aggressive and refused some of his imaginative pieces, he was reviewing for the *Nouvelle Revue Française* itself.

Before the end of 1921, however, his association with Kra had already become somewhat sporadic, if only because he had met and married Clara Goldschmidt and their "two-year-long dream" had begun. Malraux invested her dowry in stocks and shares and they traveled widely on the proceeds to Italy, Germany, Czechoslovakia, Tunisia, and elsewhere. In-between times, he read eagerly, visited galleries, mocked-up editions of erotica and other items, checked the state of their nest egg at the Stock Exchange, and spent time round the corner at the Bibliothèque Nationale in pursuance of his growing interest in archaeology and in the fabled East—which, like "adventure" itself, was much in vogue at the time. In these two years—uninterrupted by military service, since they contrived jointly to wangle him out of this obligation—he consolidated his artistic culture to a remarkable degree.

What was Malraux like at this early period? Although he was nervously rapid in speech and in movement, his intensity expressed itself as intellectuality rather than as feeling; people found him distant, not to say haughty. His vulnerability and his basic pessimism were masked by a display of confidence and determination, as well as by formal politeness—which lapsed at moments into biting sarcasm at the expense of the more ludicrous aspects of the society around him. However, there was nothing of the revolutionary about him; he was not interested in social problems as such, and merely ironical about organized politics. Again, though he found Dadaist views congenial enough, he was too independent to be bound to literary movements, and it was the self-conscious clannishness of the Surrealists, as well as their emphasis upon the unconscious, which was to lead him within a few years to see them as his "enemies." An absolutist by temperament, his early mode was that of a Nietzschean aristocratism balanced by a traditional sense of honor and by conservative prejudices deriving from his upbringing. Though he would have echoed the Surrealists' contempt for militarism and patriotism, for instance, he was far from immune to the idea of soldierly glory. On the surface, there was something of the right-wing anarchist about Malraux at this time—the more so in that he was interested less in people than in ideas and in myths.

Of these there was no shortage in this animated postwar

period, and the list of "influences" which Malraux puts forward
in an interview of 1952 is very much what the *Enquête sur les
Maîtres de la jeune littérature* of 1923 by Varillon and Rambaud would lead us to expect.[3] The more important figures are
Nietzsche, Dostoevsky, Gide, and, interestingly, the Romantic
historian Michelet, in whom he still finds "incomparable com-
prehension and generosity of heart." In addition, through Clara's
German culture, he made contact with the German Expression-
ists and with at least the general argument of Oswald Spengler's
The Decline of the West. In Dostoevsky's anguished demonstration that the unity of man could not be taken for granted, in
Nietzsche's strange ethical evolutionism and call for a new
man following upon "the death of God," in Spengler's view that
the West was in decline and that the discontinuity of civilization
cut us off from our own past, we might already seem to have
the broad lines of what was to be Malraux's "world." The impact
of such ideas upon the young writer is partly due to the fact
that they in some sense replaced a formal higher education, and
partly due to the fact that they were crystallized suddenly by
a first conflict with European order which was the more trau-
matic because it came to him in the colonized East—he read
Nietzsche at length after his arrest in Indo China, when the
whole constituted world seemed to him to be threateningly mad.

Even so, it is important to recognize that these ideas were
in the troubled air of the time and mediated through the culture in a whole variety of ways. Malraux is doubtless right to
say today that he "asserted himself for, against or through
Nietzsche just like everybody else at this period," and to suggest that this particular "influence" came to his generation
largely in transposed form through writers such as Gide. Again,
if *La Tentation de l'Occident* carries an echo of Spengler in its
title, some of its characteristic phrases could almost have come
straight from current periodicals or from the early essay *Mesure
de la France* by his own contemporary Pierre Drieu la Rochelle.
Malraux had too strong a temperament to be dependent in any
academic way upon these writers. Indeed, he was rather making
instrumental use of whatever justifying "influences" were available as he groped his way towards the momentous myth which
would transform his own underlying sense of estrangement into
the solitude of the individual in the dark night of a post-Christian

world where not only the European God had died, but European "Man." And, in the event, it is significant that the only really clear influence upon his early imaginative pieces was that of Max Jacob—from whom he could also have "derived" his view of the autonomy of art.

What importance are we to attach to these short "Cubist" pieces: *Lunes en papier, Écrit pour une idole à trompe* and *Royaume farfelu*? "None" says Malraux with cheerful finality—thus supporting W. M. Frohock's view that these semi-Surrealist tales represent a borrowed style against which the author was to revolt when he came into real conflict with the world.[4] However, Nicola Chiaramonte and more recently André Vandegans, in his massive study, have seen here rather a preoccupation with the grotesque, or *farfelu*, which continues to be a strong undercurrent in the work.[5] That Malraux should have taken a fragment of 1920 and completed and polished it for separate publication as *Royaume farfelu* in 1928, in the same year as *Les Conquérants*, might support this latter view to some extent—though he himself laughs it off by saying that this was done in the peculiar circumstances of a bout of rheumatic fever, and that he conceived it at the time as a sort of dream written by Claude Vannec, the future narrator of *La Voie royale*. In practice, however, the two views stated are not incompatible. Malraux's early estrangement led him, inflecting an existing style, to distance the world from himself by presenting it with a certain cold and even derisive irony in terms of the unreality of fable. As the game of living in the historical world became more real and more painful, this attitude was necessarily pushed into the margin.

Over the literary qualities of these rather mannered little pieces, it might be unfair to linger. However, *Royaume farfelu* in particular, of the same early inspiration as it essentially is, emphasizes sharply that Malraux's vision antecedes his career as "man of action." The cosmic ring, the pessimism, the exoticism, the violence, the insects, the image of blindness, the suffering, and the immanence of death: all are already present. And the story itself—oddly foreshadowing Vincent Berger's Eastern adventure in *Les Noyers de l'Altenburg*—shows that Malraux's basic fable of arduous adventure and defeat is already in place.

In the East, as Claude Roy puts it, he was "going to *verify* a certain number of internal images."[6]

Meanwhile, in 1923, through the indifferent play of the Stock Market, that verification was in fact at hand. The young couple came back from a boat trip up the Rhine to find themselves ruined. Since Malraux was firm in maintaining his objection to taking a job, something drastic had to be done. Putting his archaeological expertise and his desire for adventure into service, he decided that they would go to Indo China, find some ruined Khmer temple in the Cambodian bush, remove some long-abandoned statuettes, sell them in America, and continue to live comfortably for another two or three years on the proceeds.

With characteristic energy—and a certain poignant innocence which went with it—he soon had this "little salvage operation," as Clara calls it, firmly under way.[7]

II   *The Indo Chinese Rumpus*

"On December 24, 1923, towards midnight, at the very hour when the bells of the Churches of Pnom-Penh were summoning the Faithful to celebrate the anniversary of the birth of Christ, two inspectors of the Sûreté proceeded on board the Messageries Fluviales steamer arriving from Siem-Reap. . . ."[8] In its superb and majuscular pomposity, the Saigon newspaper *L'Impartial*—and impartial, as it happens, is just what it was not—points up admirably Malraux's rupture with the organized world. The tragicomedy had come to a head.

Since a whole book has been written about this Indo Chinese adventure, I shall only state the bare facts of the episode and consider briefly its impact upon Malraux himself. However I should perhaps say at once that, very thorough though Walter Langlois's account is, I feel that his generosity has led him to misplace the emphasis in certain important respects. Firstly, it is clear from the early novels themselves—and Clara Malraux has since confirmed this—that the immediate aim of the enterprise was money. Secondly, I confess that my own reading of *L'Indochine,* the newspaper later edited by Malraux and Paul Monin, is a shade less favorable than his. Thirdly, though the shocking conditions in the colony certainly made a lasting impression on Malraux, I think it misleading to suggest that

he "returned from the Far East a deeply committed social re-
former."[9] It is not just that he did nothing very spectacular to
implement his promise to go back and stir up French opinion
until his real "commitment" began some eight to ten years later
(although a sense of loyalty certainly led him to make a private
approach to the prominent Socialists Marius Moutet, future
minister for the colonies, and Léo Lagrange), but also that in
such a perspective *La Voie royale* and *Les Conquérants* would
not easily be comprehensible. After his very similar trial in the
latter novel, Garine feels not so much that society is bad, in
the sense that it could be made better, but that it is absurd
as such. It is not to be lacking in sympathy for Malraux to wish
to keep clear his situation as an artist.

Malraux, then—though his archaeological passion was real,
though there was also the pull and the prestige of Adventure,
and though he may well have thought of donating some pieces
to the Musée Guimet—was in the immediate bent on making
a killing on the soaring antiques market. He needed official
permission from the Colonial Office in Paris and from relevant
authorities in Indo China, if only to be able to commandeer
native bearers for the journey into the Cambodian bush from
Siem-Reap, the provincial town near the famous Angkor ruins.
To obtain it, he wrapped up the expedition in a mixture of
ambitious academic intentions and half-truths—notably the one
that he was rich!—and appears to have signed a document in
Hanoi agreeing not to remove such sculpture as he might
discover. He also took certain precautions; for example, Louis
Chevasson, the old school friend pressed into service to accompany them, traveled separately to Saigon and Malraux, according
to the official account, expressed great surprise at meeting him.[10]

Ironically enough, however, the authorities seem to have been
suspicious of the rather improbable young trio from the start,
and when they finally set out from Siem-Reap on December
17, 1923, one of their bearers was a police informer. Although
the project had been presented as being in part an attempt to
trace the ancient royal road linking the old imperial capital of
Angkor to the northern part of the medieval Khmer empire,
they made directly for the recently discovered temple of Banteai-
Srey, some twenty miles north as the crow flies. After with difficulty prying loose some splendid and valuable *devatas,* or

goddess figures, they came back at once to Siem-Reap. Malraux, in fact, by spending only three to four days on the trip—instead of the legendary "ten months in the bush" which we find in critical studies as late as 1967—was walking straight into a trap very largely of his own devising. Indeed, the real interest and pathos of the affair lie not in any moral innocence on his part, but in the youthful naïveté which led him to think he could outwit a mediocre world which, in reality, was indifferently allowing him enough rope with which to hang himself.

Legally, however, matters were more complicated. For one thing, the rights of French jurisdiction in this Cambodian province turned out to be very far from clear. For another, although the temple had been the subject of an official monograph, nobody had taken the elementary step needed to have it listed as a historical monument. Technically, therefore, Malraux had a good case, and the sentence of the Phnom-Penh Tribunal on July 21, 1924: three years' imprisonment for Malraux and eighteen months for Chevasson, was a savage one. That such retribution should be exacted for a youthful escapade of this kind in a colony where wholesale embezzlement and even murder had frequently gone unpunished—where, indeed, the seeds of the present Viet Nam conflict were being imprudently sown—was almost as grotesque as anything in *Royaume farfelu*. Except that now, even if he was not in fact to see the inside of a prison, it was real. Why then did it happen?

It happened partly for circumstantial reasons: because the authorities had under pressure at that very time been trying to clamp down on looting from cultural monuments, because of the private ambition of officious and unscrupulous individuals, and because of a more than usually inept police report which saw avant-garde literary activity as being tantamount to Bolshevik or Anarchist subversion! Essentially, however, it happened because Malraux, in his apparent arrogance but actual innocence, went about things in this complacent little colony in quite the wrong way.

Although he had agreed to let Chevasson take the blame so that he himself, as the more resourceful one, would be free to go to Paris to prepare an appeal should things go wrong, he conducted his own defense with enough brio to convince a dozen courts that he had orchestrated the whole venture.

Above all, by making wild claims about himself which were all too easily shown to be fictitious—and by walking, in order to make them, straight into the parlor of the unsavory editor of *L'Impartial*—he presented the prosecutor, the mediocre local press and, indeed, the press in Paris with a field day. And, given his will to independence and his vulnerability, the humiliation could only be increased by the fact that it was Clara, left free to return to Paris, who largely retrieved the situation by mustering invaluable statements of support from well-known writers—with André Breton, whom Malraux did not much like, well in the van—and by seeking the assistance of his mother as well as his father. Add to this the last straw of the loyal but "enlightened" Clara's brief affair on the boat going home and one begins to see that it is not for nothing that critics should speak of a traumatism of failure in the novels, or that he should have told Clara one day that he had a memory only for humiliations.

However, this was not the end of Malraux, but rather the beginning. He reacted. Ten days before the Appeal Court in Saigon sat at the end of September, he replied boldly to *L'Impartial*, which was trying hard to whip up opinion against him. And when his sentence was reduced to one year with stay of execution, he returned to France not just with a more heroic and by now politicized version of his condemnation, but with the firm intention of going back to avenge himself on the colonial authorities. This desire had objective justification in his eyes since he had had ample leisure to observe conditions in the colony, and had come into contact with various dissentients— notably the courageous young liberal lawyer Paul Monin, who was then contemplating starting a daily newspaper to promote racial partnership. It was agreed that Malraux should become co-editor, and he himself took the decisive steps in Paris. By January, 1925, he was back in Saigon and on June 17 *L'Indochine* appeared.

Viewed out of context, it is not an impressive paper. It looks, indeed, like a strange mixture of the Surrealist gag (such as the surreptitious insertion of a welcoming notice on the front page of the *Courrier Saïgonnais,* which then had to reassure its readers that it remained the "passionate defender of Order"!)[11]; of serious political criticism, mainly from Monin;

and of extravagant scurrility, mainly from Malraux (the editor of *L'Impartial*, villain as he clearly was, was nailed on such comparatively apolitical counts as ugliness, cowardice, personal uncleanliness, and mother beating!) The energy and delight which he put into these articles, spurred on as he was by the orchestrated fury of the governmental press to the point of keeping a gleeful tally of the rich descriptions applied to him— *Saïgon-Républicain* would have won the prize by presenting him as "straight out of the lap of André Gide, shuttling between literature, business, burglary and prostitution"![12]—show him hitting back with a vengeance. It took him some little time, to put it mildly, to attain to that consistent sobriety of tone which was perhaps the best means of promoting racial partnership and appealing to liberal opinion. But he did.

Placed back in context, and compared with the provincial dullness, pomposity, and intellectual barrenness of the other, materially more endowed Saigon newspapers, *L'Indochine* begins to look very much better. It did at least carry serious political articles and other features from France under syndication agreements with Hachette and the weekly *Candide*, and it did let in some daylight by providing adequate news about Asia in general. And when one considers the abuses which it denounced, such as the control of the press through oblique subsidies or the scandalous sales of government lands in conditions involving virtual dispossession of the peasants—indeed the general self-defeating corruption and ostrich-like conservatism of the administration, which Langlois details excellently—it begins to look like a public necessity. The brutally authoritarian Governor of Cochin China paid it a rare compliment when, having failed to bribe or browbeat Malraux, who challenged him publicly with great courage, he contrived to choke it out within two months by applying pressure on the printers.

Despite great difficulties, however, they managed to get the paper going again in reduced format and at irregular intervals —as *L'Indochine Enchaînée*—for a further twenty-three issues between November 4 and February 24, 1926. To several perfectly dignified editorials which he had already written Malraux now added further serious contributions. The hope was that the newly appointed governor of the colony, the Socialist Alexandre Varenne, might make some impression. Once he saw that Varenne was in fact the prisoner of the administration Malraux, at the end of December or early in January, left the colony: another defeat, but an honorable one.

He had been a leading force in the Young Annam League and he had joined the Kuomintang, or Chinese Nationalist party; he had been able to tell them that they had the same enemies, if not the same aims. There had been nothing very revolutionary by European standards about the views he had expressed— he had really seen himself as defending the long-term interests of the French in Indo China. He accepted the capitalist system, but argued that corruption militated against the efficient economic development of the country, that the rule of law was humanly and politically preferable to the rule of force, and that, for example, it was foolishly shortsighted to prevent young Annamites from going to France only to see them educated instead in England, the United States, or Russia. In fact, he had made his appeal in terms of an enlightened, practical liberal conservatism. Since it had failed, it was time to get back to the business of being Malraux—and a writer.

At the end of August, 1925 he had gone to Hong Kong for a few days to get new type for the paper. Paul Morand's statement that he went to Canton on this occasion—the only piece of objective testimony to the Chinese phase of the legend—has recently been ironically dismissed by Clara Malraux as a fable imposed upon the credulous Morand by her husband.[13] In fact, it now seems quite clear that Malraux did not visit mainland China before 1929 or 1931, and that this whole central dimension of the legend is fantasy.[14] Which in an important sense is all to the good, since it brings out the significant Malraux, the haunted young "dominated writer" described by Jean Prévost, if still very romantically, as follows:

He could not look you straight in the face; it was as though his glance were following some imaginary bee in every direction. His shoulders were clenched as though he had a dagger stuck in his back. His fingers were feverish, quivering, trying to loosen themselves. As soon as anyone came towards him, the gaunt face seemed more uneasy. A child who has been punished, a vulnerable rebel who as yet has loved only death: this was Malraux, back from Asia.[15]

III *Diagnosis of the West*

La Tentation de l'Occident is cast in the form of a correspon-
dence between Ling, a young Chinese visiting Europe, and
A. D., a young Frenchman visiting China. However, this is
more of a formal than a necessary dramatic device, and the
work may with due reservations be taken as a metaphysical
essay. At one level, it is a study in comparative psychology, but
since the representation of the Eastern mind is rather summary
and conventional—partly because Malraux, more clearly than
others, saw that the temptation to the West had in any event
been largely removed by the virtual destruction of Eastern
culture under the growing impact of Europe—this aspect fades
in importance. What the confrontation of East and West has
suggested to Malraux is not the superiority of one or the other,
but the arbitrariness of *each*. The emphasis falls therefore, as
in the companion essay "D'une jeunesse européenne" of 1927,
upon the sickness of Western civilization and upon the "unreality"
of the individual within it. With these two short pieces, indeed,
Malraux takes the decisive jump.

That he has not so much established a firm theoretical plat-
form as achieved a mythical projection of his own situation
emerges from his disjunctive, aphoristic rhetoric itself. He in
effect invests his own sense of estrangement with general historical and moral necessity, sees his despair as representative of
a whole generation, and shakes out the myth—the inner collapse
of a civilization and the need for a new conception of Man—
upon which the whole of his work will be built. At one level, of
course, the very boldness and lyrical consistency of this private
triumph of mythopoeic fixation will have unfortunate conse-
quences, in that Malraux as thinker will be bound to a set
of stark poetic conceptions never fully realized (or stated) in
purely intellectual terms. However, this only to say that it is an
excellent starting point for Malraux as imaginative writer.

Similarly, it is pointless to deny the originality of these essays
by suggesting that they represent an opportunist fusion of ideas
already current in the postwar period. It is true that in the
background we have the Spenglerian idea of a declining West,
the impact of Freud upon the notion of the self-determining
rational individual, the moral shock of the war and the doubts

about science and progress as indicated by Valéry—to say nothing of the new openness of European culture at this time and the vogue of speculation about the East. However, the originality lies precisely in the opportunism, and in the fusion. By its passion and its very starkness, Malraux's myth was more suggestive and influential than parallel statements such as Drieu la Rochelle's *Le Jeune Européen* or Marcel Arland's "Sur un nouveau mal du siècle."[16] Indeed, in relation to the development of French existentialism, some of his central statements as to the absurdity of European civilization are of quite historic importance. Again, if a very general Nietzschean influence is evident, he in fact puts that forerunner in his place in "D'une jeunesse européenne" by saying: "If Nietzsche finds so many echoes in despairing hearts, it is because he is himself only the expression of their despair and their violence." Concerned no longer with the "death of God" but with the "death of Man," he sees himself as being a historical stage beyond: as exploring a kind of post-Nietzschean impasse.

Although he observes sharply that the only absolute which the Eastern contemplative encounters is the extreme point of his own sensibility, Malraux's approach is nevertheless dictated by a romantically absolutist longing for a complete identity with oneself and with the cosmos which might almost seem to be opposed in principle to the idea of civilization as we know it. His historical placing of the problem, which is itself very sketchy and which clearly begs a great many questions, is briefly as follows.

As opposed to Eastern civilizations, which sought to merge man into the world and into cosmic rhythms, Western civilization from Greece onward has depended rather upon the separation of man from the world, and thus upon a tension between them. Civilization, coming therefore to mean the imposition of a *human* order upon the world, produced a race of suffering conquerors or geometers; Rome itself is eloquent for Ling of a vulgarly barbarous ideal of power which made even its own value of self-sacrifice a spiritually empty one. Now Christianity at once expressed and contained this suffering and this tension through the idea of the individual soul and that of a God both personal and collective, but the inner dynamic of Western man led him eventually to kill this God—as Oedipus defeated the

Sphinx, only to be brought face to face with the final riddle and indestructible enemy: himself. So the conqueror, after his long struggle to impose himself upon the world, in effect ends up staring at his own face in the mirror.

It is at this point in the fable that for Malraux, though he burns his own bridges in relation to Christianity with some finality, the modern rot sets in. For there followed the "religion of Humanity" of nineteenth-century agnostic humanism whereby Man himself replaced God, and this whole cultural tradition—which of course is still ours, up to this day—has in his view failed. Even before the Great War demonstrated the bankruptcy of the values of reason, progress and science (this is not so much stated as simply assumed, and the later Malraux will also sweepingly reject science on the basis of the existence of the atomic bomb), a fragmenting and increasingly decadent individualism was already driving people hopelessly back upon themselves. Once this relativistic civilization has lost the hope of finding in science the meaning of the world, it is left without a spiritual goal and loses its specificity. A sharp proof of this decline is its uneasy interest in other forms of sensibility and culture—that the Western museum should be seen as a kind of symbol of this sclerosis is interesting in view of Malraux's very different argument later on in *Les Voix du silence*. But feeling hardens into mere knowledge and the individual is left to measure the grievous gap between the deep needs of his sensibility and the empty allegories which make up his system of thought. Indeed, the despair is such that modern artists, Freudians, and Surrealists are being driven to deny not only the integrity of the personality but the very notion of reality—and on these "self-conscious and complacent follies" Malraux is severe.

European civilization, then, is an empty shell and European man unreal; indeed, doubly unreal. For, ironically, even if his God is long since dead, Christianity has in fact molded his psyche. The Christian aspirations to unity, plenitude, and responsibility still constitute the form of his sensibility, the "grid" through which he sees the world. So, dead as Christian and dead as humanist, but still wandering automatically amid the ruins like a ghostly and ludicrous mixture of both, he is left naked before the permanent fatalities—time, suffering, death—which continue ineluctably to govern human existence. More than that, he seems condemned to remain so. For in the absence of any new religion which might fall from the skies to break the deadlock, civilization could only be reconstructed on the basis of a new idea of man himself, whereas it is inherent in the situation as Malraux defines it that man, on his own terms—with sciences which are mere allegories and a psychology which is mere fable—is unknowable.

In an analysis which often anticipates that of Jean-Paul Sartre's *L'Être et le néant,* Malraux argues the impossibility of knowing other people, to a large extent in terms of the privileged relationship of love. The irony of the lover's situation, he contends, is that his love depends upon two different orders of feeling or sensation: his own, and those which he *attributes* to the other. Yet in fact he can never meet the reality of the other but only his own idea of the other: only his own expectation, only himself. The solitude of the individual, at this stage, is seen as irreducible—the more so since he is also a stranger to himself. He has a primary awareness of himself as a kind of brute "intensity," but with a mind which is the unreal derivative of a dead civilization, a perfected instrument now turning in the void, he cannot know himself objectively. And if, in despair, he attempts an independent analysis of the self, he will be led away from the general toward the arbitrariness of the particular. In any event, he cannot conceive himself with any continuity since he sees himself constantly in intentional terms and since his very memory is biased. In the broken-down theater of European civilization this decadent "individualist" is little more than a monster of wish fulfillment: he is absurd.

At the formal level, therefore, the disaster might seem to be complete. Indeed, if one were to set out to devise an objective justification for a sense of alienation one could hardly go further than this. Malraux confirms his break with the Christian tradition, but also breaks explicitly with the liberal humanism which followed it. And the emphasis on the metaphysical makes the social irrelevant; from the moment that rationalism, science and progress go by the board there is no room for Marxism, social reformism, or revolution. He denies the reality of the civilization, the reality of the individual, and the role of the mind. He says that there is no ideal for which the young European might fight. He proclaims the need for a new view of man, but appears to have left himself no values with which to move toward this. The courage born of despair may simply be blind. The irrelative "intensity" of the individual is little more than the awareness of one's organic existence, and is logically at the mercy of the chaotic, myth-making madness of the involuntary life within. The "lucidity"—which was to become a key concept for a number of writers—can only exist on a razor's edge between the absurdity within and the balancing absurdity of the civilization without, and by the terms of Malraux's own analysis it cannot be worth much. And yet it is on the basis of this paralysis that Malraux, paradoxically but inevitably, is led to gamble on the idea of "action."

For one thing, the intensity of youth and of a certain kind of temperament is its own volition. "The absence of all conviction," he told *Les Nouvelles Littéraires* in 1926, "leads some men towards passivity, and others towards extreme action."[17] For another—and this is quite an important moment in contemporary French literature, the more so since Malraux moves fortuitously into close parallel with the thought of the German philosopher Martin Heidegger—there is still one hard term of reference left. Investing the empty ruins, filling the vacuum left by the unreality of both the culture and the individual until it comes to substitute for civilization itself as the only defining reality, there is ... death. So "lucidity," which is the awareness of the absurd, moves toward "authenticity" which is the courageous attempt to make something positive of the dark destiny of "living-toward-death." And in order to actualize one's own metaphysical absurdity, to experience immediately this final reality of living with death, one needs the extreme situation. It is a despairing gamble but at least, since death is after all universal, one can try to cut through the net and live as "Man," rather than as a mere historical individual falsely particularized by a dead civilization.

Finally, there is a suggestion at the end of *La Tentation de l'Occident* that certain dark possibilities—killing, for example—may offer a chance of inflecting the irrelevant, vestigial structure of the European psyche. Can one, by moving beyond an unreal good and an unreal evil, by living fiercely and experimentally as the Nietzschean "Superman," get beyond the old complex of guilt, responsibility, and remorse and somehow smash through toward a more real perspective: see the true face of the world and of "fundamental man" at last? Perhaps not, but the tragic adventure must be attempted.

It will be attempted, not in life itself, but rather—since Malraux was essentially a writer, and busy at that time establishing himself at Gallimard's—in the double projection of his first two novels. The adventure calls for a suitably violent and distant metaphysical playground; in *La Voie royale* it will be the jungle, in *Les Conquérants* the Chinese revolution. And, as indeed the echoing irony of these titles already intimates, the quest for Man among mere men will be a somewhat desperate affair.

CHAPTER 3

The Post-Nietzschean Impasse

I The "New Man"

THERE is a sense in which Malraux's first two novels constitute his most original achievement. This originality, of course, was somewhat obscured at the time by the interest of the Chinese revolutionary background of *Les Conquérants* and by the surface exoticism of the jungle adventure of *La Voie royale*—as it has since been obscured to some extent also by a natural tendency on the part of critics to read these works in the light of his famous and more "committed" later novels. However, Malraux himself was in no doubt as to what he was attempting and there were certain other writers, such as Pierre Drieu la Rochelle and Emmanuel Berl, who discerned behind these writings an attitude which, in their eyes, was not only new but of peculiar relevance to the Europe of the late 1920s.

In an interview given to the left-wing *Monde* in 1930, Malraux says of the hero of *Les Conquérants*: "Garine represents to a high degree the tragic sense of human solitude which scarcely exists for the orthodox communist," and goes on to suggest that social revolution is no answer to the problem of death. "The essential element of *La Voie royale*," he says further, "is the projection in terms of an extremely violent situation of the fundamental solitude of man in the face of death." That the same theme should govern the presentation of "actions" so essentially different as collective revolutionary effort and private imperialism in the jungle is eloquent of the obsessional force of the death-dominated metaphysic—and, of course, of the consequent distance between Malraux and any real social or political commitment at this time. Indeed, he gets into hot water with this same interviewer when he seems to be reducing the whole moral and political interest of revolution to an excited and lyrical preoccupation with the *techniques* of insurrection, which he happily calls the "science of urbanism"!

From Malraux's point of view, these apparently rather different novels were twin projections of the same problem. And the concentration on this theme of "living-toward-death" is such as to permit only a unilinear type of fictional development and to dictate the essential similarity of these novels. We find in each the same ironic ambiguity of the title, the same story pattern, the same relationship between the young neophyte and the more experienced hero, and the same narrowing of focus upon the tragic defeat of the older hero at the hands of the world. In each, in effect, we have Malraux in double projection—in the immediate as the young apprentice man of action, in mythical extension as the mature adventurer at grips with a resistant reality: Garine and his counterpart in *La Voie royale,* Perken. Of each it could be said, as Malraux says in conversation of Perken, that he is a "fantasy character"—not so much taken from the world as invented to meet the situation of a collapse of a world, the alienated European as metaphysical adventurer facing up to the Absurd. In fact, the real interest of these novels lies in the delineation of a new type of fictional hero, and in the way in which this hero is expressive of certain disquieting tendencies of the time.

The fact that French writers were increasingly "politicized" under the impact of the grim European situation of the 1930s—polarized in terms of Right and Left—tends to conceal the extraordinary flux and confusion of the intellectual situation of the late 1920s, only a few years earlier, and to make it all too easy to simplify the careers of many writers of the time. Malraux, seen as the Communist writer and Resistance hero, and Drieu la Rochelle, seen as the Fascist driven to suicide at the end of the war to escape trial for collaboration, are cases in point. In fact, it was not for nothing that Drieu felt that the only French writer he would wish to have at his funeral was Malraux—though, ironically, Malraux was too actively and courageously engaged on the other side at the time to be available. Both men grew up as writers in the disturbed and baffling world of the 1920s and belonged to the same broad current of Nietzschean activism; indeed, the parallel between their work at this time is such that they seem almost to be "leap-frogging" each other

from book to book. And the juxtaposition of their careers brings
out an appalling double irony.

The tragedy of Drieu la Rochelle; at least in part, is that he
was led by historical events, through a real interest in social
and political matters, from a genuine European idealism toward
the Nazi version of a "heroic Europe." Malraux, on the other
hand, though in these early novels he is in fact far more profoundly than Drieu structuring at the personal level the alienation and despair which lie at the heart of fascism, was at this
time protected paradoxically by the very depth of a sense of
estrangement which precluded any immediate social or political
commitment. He was rather more intelligent than Drieu, of
course, and tougher in the end as a person. Even so, that one
should have ended up in ignominious suicide and the other
as a government minister is a sharp reminder that writing in
twentieth-century Europe has sometimes been a seriously test-
ing business.

At all events, it is not without significance that it should have
been Drieu la Rochelle who hailed Malraux in *La Nouvelle
Revue Française* in 1930 as the "New Man" posing the problem of a "new man."[1] More fully revealing of the temper of the
time, however, is a lengthy, resounding and often wildly erratic
pamphlet inspired by the portrait of Garine in *Les Conquérants*:
Emmanuel Berl's *La Mort de la pensée bourgeoise*. For him,
Garine is a "new type of man whose mere existence resolves
many problems and difficulties"—even if this leads only to the
conclusion that "to go without knowing where is the first and
only nobility in thought and in life."[2] By its very confusion,
Berl's book is a telling statement of the disorientation of the
intellectual, paralyzed between an American capitalism dis-
credited by the depression and a Russian communism which
he feels to be no more than "an aggravated capitalism," and
vulnerable to the temptation of the flamboyant and paroxysmal
"action" which might seem somehow to break the deadlock.
Particularly remarkable is his statement, however romantic, of
the sense of isolation and hopelessness of the intellectual at
this time: "Alone in relation to the world, to himself, to his
wife, to his job, alone in friendship, alone between the urinals
and the ruins, alone amid the ominously cracking sounds of this

universe to which he clings, but which he knows to be condemned."[3]

Malraux's emphasis on solitude is essentially metaphysical, of course, but one begins to see how it could have seemed to relate to the actual historical and social situation of this Europe of the lull before the storm. Indeed, against this background and in the context of his career as a whole, the essential interest of these two novels is that in trying to get beyond the paralysis expressed in the early essays he does indeed portray a kind of "new man"—and that this new man may be said dispassionately to bear a strong resemblance to Fascist man. Since his more famous work of the 1930s will be an attempt to break out of this position toward collective, humane values, this early stage is an important one. I shall therefore deal briefly with the general features of each of the two novels in turn, and then concentrate upon the contradictions of this "new man."

Although *La Voie royale* was written after *Les Conquérants,* it represents a momentary step back to the first and "purer" phase of the adventurer in that Malraux wrote it as a tragic prologue to a series of novels about collective action to be entitled *Puissances du désert*—the series being dropped simply because, as he says, "the continuation turned into *La Condition humaine*." It is therefore at once more convenient and truer to the movement of his development to consider *La Voie royale* first.

II   La Voie royale

La Voie royale is a highly intensified fictional projection of the archaeological expedition—the exploration of the ancient Khmer Royal Road stretching northward from Angkor, across the Dang Raek mountains, into Siam—of which Malraux had dreamed, but which he had not in fact carried out. The young Claude Vannec, alienated from Europe and financially ruined, is on his way to the East to play this "last card." Driven as he is by the "austere domination of death," he feels that the wealth gained from the sculpture he may find in the abandoned temples will at least give him the freedom to "choose his enemies" and to live out his revolt on his own terms. On the ship, he has already recognized a kindred spirit in the legendary but aloof

Perken, a *heimatlos* European adventurer who has in the past acted as a semiofficial maverick agent in the interior for the Siamese government—the books opens mysteriously with a taut discussion about eroticism in which Perken propounds the view that "it is essential *not to know* one's partner" but to treat her simply as "the other sex." Already warned of the near-impossibility for a white man of accomplishing his jungle expedition on his own, Claude attempts to enlist him in the enterprise and Perken, for his own reasons, accepts.

Like Claude, Perken is obsessed by death, though he feels that the real death is *déchéance*: the decay of the will and of the sense of one's metaphysical absurdity through the acceptance of the fictive values of civilization and through the wear and tear of time, both on oneself and on those one has loved. The resulting impossibility for him of living in society, or even inside normal relationships, has led him to try to "gamble against his death" by leaving "a scar on the map." For fifteen years he has been maneuvering to take over a whole tract of the mountainous interior, draw together a score of tribes into one private state, await the inevitable battle with Siam itself and with the surrounding countries—and thus enshrine himself in the memory of many men. This public defiance of the world combines with a more private expression of the lust for power and for "revenge against the universe": the denial of the personality of others, as represented by the possession of women. He has mastered the erotic cults of the natives to the extent that he can almost feel himself to *be* the woman; that is, the woman as dominated by himself. However, after these fifteen years—and a sharp reminder of the inevitable final impotence, administered in a brothel during the stop at Djibouti—he now wants what he calls "peace."

He will settle for the highland region of his election, arm his wild tribesmen, and protect his way of life against the encroaching railway and the general advance of civilization until he dies. If he now accepts Claude's proposition, it is largely because he needs money for machine guns, but also because he is anxious to find and, if necessary, eliminate the ex-legionary Grabot: a primitive version of the adventurer type who has vanished mysteriously in a neighboring part of the bush and whom he suspects of attempting to queer his pitch with the natives. So the two men eventually set out together from Siem-Reap, being driven farther and farther into the jungle as they encounter only empty temples until at last they find a decorated one and remove the sculpture. At this point the native leader of the caravan, a spy planted by the French authorities which Claude has defied, causes their bearers to desert. Unable to turn back, they are forced up into savage Stieng country where, after concluding an uneasy truce, they await the appearance of Grabot, whom Perken imagines to be in control of their fate.

But Grabot has been taken captive, blinded, and reduced to a mindless beast of burden yoked to a treadmill—an ironical image of "fundamental man" suggesting at once the human situation and the fragility of civilization. They release him, thus breaking the truce, and wait while the warriors prepare to attack their hut. In the end Perken, "driven sexually towards this liberty-in-death," advances across the compound, ambiguously attracted at once by the will to defy torture and the fascination of torture itself. Although he falls on a war-dart, he contrives to gain freedom for Claude and himself through a subterfuge and the promise of a great quantity of trinkets, even if he reverts to a "hatred of life" once his hysteria has lapsed. The two men now make their way down to the first Siamese township, where an opium-ridden English doctor tells Perken with brutal authority that he is going to die like a dog of the wound in his knee. Claude, temporarily abandoning his sculpture—and exalting this fairly elementary act of loyalty as something which sets him apart from the great mass of men—offers to accompany him on his last painful journey up to his own "kingdom." As they set out, in a losing race against the advancing railroad and the military column which will not only free Grabot but pacify the whole region, Perken fights to wrest a grandiose moral victory from this "monstrous defeat" by actively *living* his dying, by attempting the ultimate paradox of turning this imposed death into a free act.

It was not an easy task to embody a metaphysical fable in an adventure story and, without accepting the severity of Malraux's own view that *La Voie royale* was a "botched job," one may well feel that he did not entirely succeed in giving tragic force to this presentation of living-toward-death. To some extent the reasons for this are technical. He does not

maintain the narrative point of view with as much rigor as in
Les Conquérants, there are some awkwardly inserted discussions and background passages, and the writing is unequal
and sometimes overexplicit. The novel seems to fall between
two stools, in that it is felt to be either overstylized in part or
not sufficiently stylized throughout—the adventurers never once
eat a meal, for example, though a great deal of other practical
detail is given. Nevertheless, the decisive reason is that the
main characters do not quite possess enough stature to stand
convincingly for "Man."

It is not so much that we are necessarily in a world of outlaws, where the only values are courage (the alienated hero's
preparedness to suffer in order to challenge an absurd and
hostile world) and loyalty to one's fellow outlaws—though the
loyalty is limited and appears to come to Claude as something of
a revelation. However, since formal society, in the person of
the director of the French Institute with his symbolical abscess
of the liver, is discarded along with the false solution of the
opium-ridden doctor, the book depends morally upon Claude-
Perken-Grabot as the three stages of the adventurer-hero. Now
Grabot is a largely symbolical and primitive character, while
the excessively nervous behavior of Claude seems to veer too
readily toward the hysterical or the merely childish. The creation of Perken himself—seen by one seasoned reviewer as
being "absolutely new"[4]—is very successful; indeed he is a
kind of tragically estranged version of that "new man, happy
and proud, to whom it will be indifferent to live or not live"
announced by Dostoevsky in *The Possessed.* Even so, the very
similarity between the adventurers, and notably the suggestion
of sexual abnormality about all three, does tend to give the
impression of the triple projection of a special psychological
case as much as of a universal metaphysical problem.

Nevertheless, the novel remains an extremely interesting one.
Several of the chapters are excellently conducted, the descriptive writing often glitters with a hard lyricism, and there is some
splendid observation of details and textures in the jungle scenes
in particular. Indeed the rendering of this threatening, swarm-
ing, disintegrating "gangrene" is a considerable tour de force—
the original, in some sense, to which Sartre's presentation of the
"otherness" and "viscosity" of things in *La Nausée* constitutes

the ironic suburban pendant. The jungle is at once a powerfully concrete presence and a powerfully polyvalent symbol. Its hostility is that of the world to the vengeful, alienated thirst for power; its thriving antheaps are an ironical answer to the social "antheap" from which the heroes are trying to escape; its perpetual decomposition is the image of *déchéance*; its "madness" and that of the strange humans it harbors mirror the inner "madness" of the European psyche dominated only by the adventurer's despairing will. And "madness" meets "madness" with grim irony and finality when, at key points in the novel, the "lucid" will flogs itself on to the point of hysteria—and Claude or Perken can only meet the "inhuman" jungle with the "inhuman" in themselves. There is no way through this web. The indifferent ascendancy of the jungle, and the *impersonality* of the death which it imposes, are measured in the end.

III Les Conquérants

Billed as "a new conception of the novel," banned in the Soviet Union and in Italy, and analyzed at length by the exiled Trotsky—who found the work remarkable, but discerned no great "natural affinity" between Malraux and the Revolution and thought he would have benefited from a "good dose of Marxism"[5]—*Les Conquérants* made more impact than *La Voie royale* and is also the better novel.

Of course, by the time he was writing this later "tragic prologue" to the projected *Puissances du désert* Malraux was already in an awkward transitional stage: at once going back to a simpler phase of the adventurer-hero in Perken and groping forwards toward a style which might sustain a larger view of the human situation—as it was to turn out, in *La Condition humaine*. At all events, the earlier *Les Conquérants* is technically more controlled, while the dilemma of the estranged "new man" emerges the more poignantly when the "jungle" confronting him is a significant moment of immediate history: the revolutionary situation in Canton and the Hong Kong strike of 1925.

Since *La Condition humaine* deals with the decisive rupture within the Chinese revolutionary movement of 1927, less than two years later, this common background should perhaps be indicated at once. It is not easy to do so briefly, given the almost unbelievably chaotic situation of this old and isolationist society which had long since lost its coherence and was being modernized from without by competing expansionist powers, including Great Britain, France, the United States, the Soviet Union, and Japan. Outside the territorial "concessions" of these powers, the country was fragmented under the rule of a large number of greater or lesser generals or "warlords," some sustained and manipulated by one or other foreign interest, others operating independently as simple bandits. With alliances between these parties shifting continually, fighting went on intermittently across the country. And through this veritable Chinese puzzle of a situation Dr. Sun Yat-sen's Chinese Nationalist party, or Kuomintang—which, under the leadership of General Chiang Kaishek, was to rule the country until driven into exile by the victorious Communists in 1949—was painfully emerging as the first nationally unifying force in modern China.

Sun himself was a converted Christian and a broadly democratic nationalist, who had become provisional president of the newly declared Republic of China after the overthrow of the effete Manchu dynasty in 1911. Without control of the army he had soon found himself powerless, and was driven back into the wilderness as the Peking government reverted to shifting combinations of warlords backed by the Western powers. In 1920, however, he managed to set up an opposition government at Canton, in the south. His aim was now to develop this new base, forge an army strong enough to march northwards against Peking, and create a unified Chinese Republic. To do so he needed help and, having received no encouragement from the West, he made an agreement with Soviet Russia in 1923.

This led to a working partnership between the Kuomintang and the small Chinese Communist party which, though it obviously intended to take over the eventual control of the whole movement, agreed to subordinate itself to overall Kuomintang authority. More immediately important, it led to the arrival of Michael Borodin with a professional group of political and military advisers attached to the Communist International, or "Comintern." Borodin restructured the whole Kuomintang party, while the chief Soviet military adviser General Galen set up a military academy for training the necessary officers at

Whampoa, the command of which was given to the brilliant young Chiang Kai-shek. It is in the context of the impetus thus given to anti-imperialist and potentially revolutionary agitation that the tactical struggle in Canton in 1925 presents itself —with the further complicating factor that Sun Yat-sen had just died and that the latent dissensions within the Kuomintang itself, which were to lead to Chiang's break with the Communists at Shanghai in 1927, were already coming to the surface.

To present so complex a situation to a European audience in successful fictional form would have challenged any young writer attempting his first novel. For Malraux—and the merits of the work as well as its billing as a "new conception of the novel" may be seen more fully in this light—it set quite peculiar problems, and in two distinct ways.

To begin with, not only was he ideologically uncommitted but he was not primarily concerned with the Chinese situation as such. He was using it as a foil in an attempt to give something approaching mythical stature to his new kind of Outsider turned tragic "man of action." He was therefore in the somewhat paradoxical position of having to deal with collective political action in China in such a way as to bring out the essentially individual, metaphysical, *European* drama of a revolutionary leader working with the Comintern who regards Marxism as "doctrinaire nonsense," and whose activity springs not from hope but from absolute despair.

Malraux contrives to do this plausibly in a variety of ways. Knowing that he can always convince his European audience by a telling use of detail, he boldly gives his Garine a leading importance—even representing him as having organized the Whampoa Military Academy—which no such European "adventurer" could have possessed. He also uses a three-part construction to serve the same end. In *Les Approches* he establishes the background economically from the outside so that, after showing Garine's tactical struggle with Hong Kong and a British-backed warlord, he can focus upon the personal tragedy of the lonely and probably dying individual in his final part, entitled *L'Homme*. More generally, he contrives successfully to subordinate the revolutionary situation to the terms of Garine's personal revolt by placing it in the perspective of the European impact on China. At the political level he empha-

sizes the tactical struggle between the Comintern and British
influence, but he also offers as the metaphysical meaning of
the rebellious spirit in this old society now breaking up under
Western influence the growth of a European type of individualism. The terrorist Hong, in particular, incarnates this discovery
of the particularity and the simple shortness of the individual
life—and the consequent anger that it should be vitiated by
poverty and injustice.

This emphasis was in fact necessary to Malraux if he was to
succeed in giving his hero general tragic significance. For one
thing, the foils to Garine need not be too specifically Chinese.
The practical, down-to-earth Borodin (Borodine in French) is
of course a Russian, while the right-wing Kuomintang idealist
conservative and upholder of nonviolence, Tcheng-Daï, is presented as a sort of Chinese Gandhi and is more of a general
moral type than a national one. More profoundly, even if he is
at odds with Marxism and not tied humanly to the Chinese
revolution, the alienated Garine can thereby seem to be closer
in spirit to the human meaning of that revolution than any
organizing bureaucrat of the Comintern.

The second major problem facing Malraux when he sat down
to write Les Conquérants was even more formidable. He could
hardly argue starkly that European civilization was meaningless and then proceed as if the novel—with its "omniscient
author," its "well-rounded characters" and other conventions—
did not itself participate in the Absurd. The weakness of La
Voie royale is largely due to the fact that he was by then moving back uneasily toward the traditional form. Here, in his
"new conception of the novel," he meets the difficulty head on.

His metaphysic logically requires him to present experience
in urgently direct and unmediated form. In order to suppress
the "omniscient author," he uses a narrator and develops a
kind of behaviorist impressionism, writing in the present tense
in a tersely notational or telegraphic style which is very effective.
He constructs cinematically, moving from one scene to the
next by means of a suspended shot or fadeout. His use of head-
lines and radio flashes, in a manner reminiscent of Dos Passos,
adds to this dramatic immediacy. His insistence on documentary
evidence, even if it leads to some awkwardness, fits in ironically
with the sad discovery of the romantic Garine that the war he

is fighting is the new and sedentary one of reports and telephone messages. The risks Malraux is running are obviously that the role of the narrator can not always be made plausible and that characters other than Garine may well seem flat—and both of these criticisms could justifiably be made. But the rewards of boldness and rigor are won through a painterly eye for significant detail and a characteristic skill in using effects of sound and silence, light and shade. In this remarkable first novel he does indeed achieve the poignant immediacy necessary to give stature to his estranged hero.

For Garine there is not only "no strength but no *real life*" without the haunting conviction that the world is meaningless. His alienation having been reinforced by the humiliation of having been tried for aiding abortion—a transference of Malraux's own trial—he finds the very idea of human society absurd. And yet this man, by a tragic irony, is engaged in promoting social revolution while yet knowing that he is not at one with the people whom he is serving, that the social order he is trying to create will certainly reject him, and that malaria and dysentery are destroying him—as surely as the poison from the war-dart was destroying Perken on his grim death march up to his pathetic illusion of a forest kingdom.

The contradiction of Perken was that his revolt against European values led him to become in fact the crudest kind of Western adventurer-imperialist. The contradiction of Garine, apart from the fact that he is fighting against Europe in the East alongside Comintern men implementing a Marxist philosophy which he must regard as nineteenth-century European nonsense, is that his alienation finds compensation in a thirst for power which cannot harness itself to clear or satisfying ends. He cannot achieve a cause. In the end, the sick "revolutionary" is toying deliriously with the idea of switching sides, of going back to the might of Western empire. The irony is that both men are tied antithetically to Europe still, and even die because of it. Their alienation is itself a European sickness.

IV *The Contradictions of the "New Man"*

The ambiguities of the "New Man," thus embodied in twin projection by Malraux on the basis of his grim analysis of Western civilization in *La Tentation de l'Occident,* may seem pretty obvious and even rather garish today. And yet the intellectual and moral confusion of the late 1920s was such that he could fairly successfully offer these heroes as having general tragic significance. As we have seen, they did indeed arouse a strong answering echo in many of his contemporaries, and not simply because there was in France a cult of adventure and of the East at this time.

Malraux was in fact probing close to the heart of the whole malaise brought about by uncertainty as to established values after World War I, and reinforced at the end of the decade by the world economic depression. He was formulating a new moral distress and adumbrating possible new attitudes. He was also, through the influences bearing upon his work—Nietzsche, Dostoevsky, Spengler—helping to crystallize the "new" or "alternative" European intellectual tradition now coming to the fore as a result of this malaise, and to which one may broadly apply the term "Existentialist." His work not only strikingly parallels that of Heidegger but clearly anticipates certain features of Sartre and Camus—whose *L'Étranger,* indeed, might have owed something to the trial in *Les Conquérants.* Even if the idea of the Absurd was not entirely new to French literature, Malraux gave it wider currency through the larger audience enjoyed by the novel and himself laid down the vocabulary of revolt, with its "lucidity" and "authenticity." The "New Man," in a word, is of some originality and historic importance.

If we attempt briefly to abstract from these early writings of Malraux a working model of this potentially dangerous prototype, we find that his various phases add up to a curious kind of vicious circle.

Although his alienation from European civilization and from the social world at large is offered as having general validity, there is nevertheless a shadow over him from the start. For his estrangement is not simply a philosophical position; it goes hand in hand with extreme nervous intensity and constant obsession. Is he simply a special psychological case? Both Claude and Perken are described as being sexually "irregular," while there are disquieting hints in *Les Conquérants* that there are certain types of damaged personalities who *cannot* accept the ordinary run of life. Again, the idea of a particular humiliation at the hands of society appears to be important. At the center of the ailing Garine's feverish recollection of scenes expressive of the humiliation of the individual through blind, ceremonial, primitively mad collective manifestations, there is the obsessional memory of his own trial. Is the estrangement of the "New Man" basically a private psychological necessity, the Absurd a rationalization of a failure to resolve the trauma of a particular defeat, the "lucidity" with which he accepts his alienation simply a function of that alienation itself?

For the point about the New Man is that he *opts* for his estrangement. Perken knows that he is "separated," while Garine decides brutally that "his life does not interest" him. Supported implicitly by Malraux's myth of the "death of Man," the New Man elects a "passion born of despair" and attempts to live a kind of vengeful antilife in terms of the will, as a fierce metaphysical gamble. He may be aware, like Garine, that this gambling is less a matter of choice than of a "private fatality," but the gambling has its own dynamic and he will attempt to ride the fatality and live it as choice. To do anything else, and in particular to commit suicide, would be fraudulent and "inauthentic."

To begin with, his situation is frightening. For now that the mediating warmth of the social has been discarded, he is brought sharply and nakedly up against his ultimate metaphysical situation: the great and final fact of death, and its indifferent, relentless everyday instrument which is time. Living is "dying." The knowledge leads him to a heightened awareness of his own nervous intensity and bodily drives: he apprehends power or the will to face torture in explicitly sexual terms. For the gambler has only two cards in his hand, his own youth and sexual capacity, and he knows that these will not be effective for long.

In this situation, he lives in a kind of controlled panic. His "intensity" needs continuity, needs projection. Hence "action." Any large action will do, as Garine knows, so long as it is continuous and absorbs all the energy. It is the idiom of action that counts rather than its meaning; it is *acting*; it is a role. Borodine, we are told, is the "man of action" proper, Garine "a man capable of action—on occasion." For the man of action operates in terms of a belief in the reality of the relative world. Our gambler, operating obsessively in starkly finalist metaphysical terms, jumps straight into the romantic and lonely role of Hero.

Since the Hero, as Perken puts it, "needs a state to gamble with," he at once—innocently and quite unquestioningly—becomes the Leader. He has no love for other men any more than for himself, he feels he must assert himself against other men, but since other men exist in the same world he will *lead* other men—justifying his role through the constant Malraux value of "effectiveness." He chooses his foreign country and his form of action, and plays to his own rules. Accepted moral standards are disowned as artificial restraints belonging to false social forms, remorse is brutally discarded and there is even, from Garine, a grave and formal rejection of simple pity. If the New Man thus places himself beyond Good and Evil it is because his ultimate metaphysical drive is somehow, independently of social forms and against time, to establish the *general* validity of his own particularity, to justify his antilife, to attain what Perken apprehends as "his revenge against the universe, his liberation from the human state."

The instrumental experiences appropriate to such a momentous enterprise are necessarily paroxysmal and antisocial: power, suffering, erotic domination, and killing. Under pressure, and in order to maintain his own image, the New Man will kill. He is, indeed, tempted to explore a *theory* of killing. For Garine, there is a serious defect in the great Russian novelists in that they show their murderers suffering from remorse, whereas he would rather expect the killer's world to be so transformed by his act as to lead him far beyond remorse. In the end, the terms "gambler," "hero," "actor," leader" merely describe aspects of what the New Man essentially is. Perken describes life as a "raw material," while Garine, speaking of his political action, says that he would have liked "to sculpt all that like wood." The New Man's intransigently plastic approach to life, his relentless pursuit of what is specific to his own intensity, his rejection of established forms, stamp him out ultimately as a kind of misplaced *artist*.

The poignancy of his situation in the novels springs from the fact that, for all his courage and determination, he must inevitably fail. The play in which he has involved himself turns out to be all too real. The relative world mangles him by forcing him to serve, by making him dependent on others, by killing him through disease. His chosen ways of heroic self-assertion, whether suffering or erotic domination, do not lead to any new world beyond; they lead only to moral hysteria, self-hatred, and failure. And, at bottom, he knows from the beginning that he must fail. Garine knows that the revolution will replace him and that he is bringing death upon himself by not leaving the tropics, as Perken knows before the action even begins that a life based on eroticism and power is doomed by the onset of impotence and the impersonal advance of railways and civilization. It is not only in Perken's final attempt to possess his death that we feel that the New Man is secretly conniving at his own death. Even if "being-toward-death" is seen resolutely as "being-*against*-death," this is little more than a self-defeating quibble; death still calls the tune and the final apotheosis for a man who writes off his own life can only lie in death. The New Man never escapes the ambiguity from which he starts. There is about him enough awareness of his own self-deception to suggest a half-conscious enactment of defeat.

The post-Nietzschean adventure of the first phase of Malraux's writing runs into an impasse. The real "destiny" of the adventurer is his very elevation of his own estrangement into a false and separatist notion of Destiny. His "authenticity" is alienation; his "lucidity," self-deception. In these circumstances, his relentless implementation of his own will "beyond Good and Evil" reveals him as a kind of noble image of Fascist man, attempting to resolve despair in a violent imperializing dream. And yet for Malraux as a writer the very representation of the New Man, and of his defeat, was something of a moral achievement and a clarification. In his next novel, *La Condition humaine*, he will attempt to find values meaningful for all men, whether they be heroic and "authentic' or not.

Positively, this corresponds to greater maturity and to a deepening of his own sympathies. Negatively, however, it corresponds—now that the dark hope represented by the early adventurer has been dashed—to the generalizing of his own despair. He may have recognized the failure of heroic individualism, but he still places primacy on individual solitude. He is still tied to the idea of Destiny, and to his view of the basic dichotomy within the personality which makes knowledge and human relationships practically impossible; the central symbol of *La Condition humaine* will be the failure of Kyo to recognize his own voice from a recording. Moving outwards toward collective values, he is still held back by his stark tendency to define life in terms of death. He is ready, in a sense, to involve the whole of humanity in his own despair.

In order to do so, he submerges the whole "new" tradition of Nietzsche, Spengler, and Dostoevsky in the older European tradition of Pascal—and sets his scene in modern Asia. The defeats and aspirations of Chinese revolutionaries of the generation of Mao Tse-tung and Chou En-lai are placed grimly under the sign of the famous *pensée* from which he takes his immensely ambitious title:

Do but imagine a number of men in chains, all condemned to death, from whom some are taken each day to be butchered before the eyes of the others. Those who remain see their own plight in that of their fellows and, looking at one another in hopelessness and grief, await their turn. In this image you see the human condition.[6]

CHAPTER 4

Pascal and Chou En-lai:
La Condition humaine

I   *The Problem of* La Condition humaine

ALMOST from the moment it was awarded the Goncourt
Prize for 1933, Malraux's next and most famous novel was
accepted as a modern European classic. Its immediate impact
was considerable and it continued to be an important term of
reference, even a formative work, for several generations of
young intellectuals. It was a novel which seemed to many to
justify its ambitious title and to be getting to the root of things.

Not only were the spectacular and bloody events with which
it dealt, Chiang Kai-shek's break with the Communists at Shanghai in 1927, of considerable historical and ideological interest in
themselves. Malraux's account was felt to have unusual authority in that he was widely believed to have been a participant.
And this authority could only be enhanced by what was clearly
a large-scale attempt to pose the meaning of these recent events
in terms of the larger European tradition; its "Communist"
activism everywhere carried echoes of Pascal, Nietzsche, Laclos,
Dostoevsky. The moment of its appearance, again, was almost
disturbingly apt. If the burning alive of political opponents
and the removal of gold teeth from the victims could still seem—
a decade before the heyday of Auschwitz and Buchenwald—
relatively non-European and exotic, there were those who
sensed in this violence something darkly prophetic.

It is indicative at once of the confusion of the period and of
the real ambiguity of the book that it should have been very
differently interpreted. On the one hand, we have the Socialist
leader Léon Blum holding it up at a political rally as a lesson
in revolutionary determination. At the other extreme, we find
the Italian *Nuova Antologia* writing about the heroic aspect of

61

the work as follows: "Death is not seen as the lamentable index to the smallness of man, but as the mirror of value, the radiance of his glory. . . . It is easy to see how such a view of life and of its value contrasts sharply with the quietest, pacifist view which is that of France today. In many ways it comes close to the very conception of Fascist doctrine."[1] The abiding interest of "classic" novels often seems to lie in a certain irreducible mystery or ambiguity. Malraux's novel of revolution, certainly, is no exception.

At the immediate moral level he has taken a decisive step forward in that the "New Man" of the first phase has now been recognized as Fascist, and rejected. He becomes the brutal counter-revolutionary Ferral, in a word, while the moral balance shifts toward revolutionaries such as Kyo and Katow, who seek their own meaning in communion with others. At the philosophical and ultimate moral level, however, Malraux's position is if anything more deeply self-contradictory than before, and the ambiguity of the work springs from its strange combination of conflicting perspectives.

His admirer Emmanuel Berl discerned the change at once when he wrote: "*Les Conquérants* sounded like a fanfare, *La Condition humaine* sounds like resignation."[2] What we had in the early novels was a rather brutal form of Nietzschean individualist self-assertion within a broad Spenglerian perspective of the decline of the West. What we now find is a nobler kind of Nietzschean attempt at self-transcendence in terms of collective values, but within a similar perspective darkened almost to blackness by a new and all-involving Pascalian pessimism. The whole dilemma emerges sharply from the most famous scene of the novel, where Malraux makes a rather desperate attempt to realize poetically a new sense of fraternity, but in a starkly hopeless situation of men waiting for inescapable torture and execution which is a direct translation into action of Pascal's appalling metaphor of the human situation. The intensity and the lyricism of the novel proceed from the fact that Malraux, striving toward a new hope, must somehow wrest it from increased despair.

Inevitably, therefore, there is a constant tension in the work: between the optimism implicit in social revolution and Malraux's metaphysical pessimism; between the reality of the his-

torical world and his stark view of Destiny; between the hope
of fraternity and the insistence on solitude; between the ideal of
dignity and the emphasis on physical and moral suffering; between the aspiration to a feeling of oneness with oneself and
his continuing view of a tragic division within the personality
which makes a man unable to know himself or other people.
The central importance of this last aspect is brought out at the
end of *Les Voix du silence,* where he writes: "We know that
we do not apprehend ourselves as we apprehend the world
outside us, and that each is to himself a monster of fantasy-
fulfillment. I once told the story of a man who fails to recognise his own voice from a recording, because he is hearing it
for the first time from the outside, through his ears, rather than
from inside, through his throat. And because it is only through
the throat that our inner voice comes to us, I called this book
La Condition humaine."

The important thing about this novel for Malraux was what
he today, in conversation, broadly calls the "Pascalian aspect."
The clearest statement of this emphasis, as it happens, is the
"blurb" accompanying the first advertisement for the novel in
La Nouvelle Revue Française of June 1933. Since Malraux was
working for Gallimard he probably drafted the passage himself, and would certainly have approved it. Translated rather
directly at the cost of some awkwardness, it runs as follows:

No man can endure his own solitude. Whether by means of love,
fantasy, gambling, power, revolt, heroism, comradeship, opium,
contemplation or eroticism, it is against this fundamental *Angst,*
consciously or not, that the characters of this novel—Communists,
Fascists, terrorists, financiers, adventurers, police chiefs, opium addicts, artists, and the women with whom they are involved—are
defending themselves, engaged as they are to the point of torture
and suicide in the Chinese Revolution, upon which for some years
depended the destiny of the Asiatic world and perhaps that of
the West.

The final phrase here reads as something of a flourish. The
Chinese Revolution, as the passage suggests, is less the subject
of the novel than the occasion, or backcloth. It provides the
extreme situation of violence and suffering—or almost provides
it, for Malraux in fact tends to add to the violence—in which

the stark, ultimate drama of "living-toward-death" may be played out. The overwhelming emphasis is clearly metaphysical, and the pivot of the work the ontological loneliness of every individual. The consequent subordination in a novel of revolution of the social, moral, and political levels is the measure of Malraux's problem, which indeed emerges from the above in almost comical fashion. For the expectant left-wing reader glancing eagerly at this advertisement in 1933 might just have been tempted to wonder whether an overall approach to the Chinese Revolution so grandly "Pascalian" as to lump together such disparate pursuits as love, gambling, and contemplation—to say nothing of Communists, financiers, and opium addicts—did not run some slight risk of blurring certain necessary political and moral distinctions: of being more "profound" than sensible and more rhetorical than real.

It is not just that Malraux has borrowed from Pascal a title, or a central symbolical scene. The fact is that his view of Destiny has merged not only with Pascal's pessimistic view of the human situation but with his idea of the *divertissement*: the activity or the mode of life which man adopts in his pathetic attempt to conceal from himself the wretchedness of his condition. If revolutionary heroism can be put on a par with gambling or eroticism in the passage quoted above, it is because this perspective tends obviously to eclipse normal differences between good and bad by placing all forms of action in the world on the same sad level as the countless forms of self-deception—the most telling phrase in the paragraph quoted is "consciously or not" (*qu'ils le veuillent ou non*). And the novel is actually constructed, very deliberately, on the principle of the equality of *divertissements* or compensatory attitudes. It is not simply a unilinear tragic novel centering around the revolutionary heroism of Kyo and Katow.

For such characters as Kyo's contemplative father Gisors, the engaging "mythomaniac" Clappique, or Ferral's mistress Valérie, are obviously too highly developed to be merely subsidiary. Again, the epilogue—in which Ferral, beaten in Paris, concludes that the bloody events in Shanghai had been "totally meaningless," and in which Gisors by refusing to go to Moscow in effect denies the terms in which his son Kyo had lived and died—casts an ironical shadow over the heroism of the revolutionaries.

Malraux, rereading Aeschylus at this time and brooding over the problem of turning *each* character into a separate destiny spinning on its own axis, was attempting a *multiple* tragedy. His private preference may go to Kyo and Katow but, artistically, he is concerned with constructing a kind of Pascalian planetarium which will as far as possible allow equal importance to the revolutionary, the antirevolutionary, the lover, the erotico-religious terrorist, or the clown, as being the different modes of solitary "living-toward-death." It was after all not for nothing that he called his latter-day "Everyman" *La Condition humaine*.

Malraux's problem, therefore, emerges as a formidable one. With greater maturity, he was striving toward collective values. He was attempting, in the marriage of Kyo and May, to create a real and convincing relationship of love. He was writing just before the birth of his first child, and the theme of the parental relation now enters the work for good. More than that, he was writing with real feeling for the suffering of the Chinese: for "those who have worked sixteen hours a day since childhood, a people of sores, scoliosis and famine." An almost anguished hunger for fraternity is discernible at moments. But how is he to represent it convincingly in a novel *based* on the idea of solitude and illusion? How is he to achieve positive values in a novel *conceived* in terms of a stark Pascalian perspective which makes value distinctions and the whole human world seem illusory and trivial? The task is tantamount to the squaring of a circle.

At the philosophical level, it cannot finally be done. However, at the artistic level, through a quite extraordinary technical achievement, Malraux contrives to contain the contradiction in such a way as to invest his novel with a continuing, challenging mystery. And the first step obviously, as he approaches his revolutionary situation, is to subordinate politics to metaphysics, or history to "Destiny."

II   *Politics as Destiny*

The situation in terms of which Malraux was projecting his view of the "human condition"—Chiang Kai-shek's break with the Communists in the spring of 1927, and the failure of the Comintern in China—is an important turning point in the history of this century. It is to a large extent at the root of the peculiar nature of Chinese communism, and even of the present political and doctrinal differences between Peking and Moscow. For the Chinese Communists, after further abortive uprisings, were soon driven into the wilderness. The movement developed thereafter in the face of much misunderstanding and mistrust on the part of Stalin, and it was as the result of a peasant rather than the classical proletarian revolution that Mao Tse-tung finally emerged victorious from his "Long March" to wrest power from Chiang Kai-shek in 1949. Malraux's political gloss on this defeat of 1927 also raises implicitly the problem which for many historians and political theorists is the most interesting one in this situation: the question of whether Stalin or his opponent Trotsky was right.

We have seen, in connection with *Les Conquérants*, that after Sun Yat-sen's death in 1925 the division within the Kuomintang was already coming to the surface. The dramatic success of the campaign to defeat the northern warlords and bring down the Peking government, launched from Canton in July 1926, could only add to the strains of this cold and wary marriage of convenience. For the Communist Left represented essentially the *social* claims of a deprived proletariat and a traditionally debt-ridden peasantry, whereas the majority of the military and political leaders of the Kuomintang in effect represented the *nationalist, antiforeign* feeling of the rising middle classes; many of these leaders were themselves dependent upon the existing rural system. By September, the army had captured the important industrial center of Hankow—which Borodin turned into a Leftist capital to balance an earlier anti-Communist coup by Chiang—and was therefore halfway to Peking. But this very advance, and above all the Kuomintang propaganda preceding it, had brought an enthusiastic peasantry to the edge of social revolution, which Chiang did not want.

Was Stalin to risk making his bid at once, and encourage this peasant revolt even against the Kuomintang? He decided, hesitantly, to damp it down and to try to keep the alliance together until Peking had been captured, or at least Shanghai. The military campaign was going well, and he badly wanted to see the country unified. For one thing, he considered it of immediate strategic importance to the new Soviet Russia that the Western imperialist hold on Asia should be weakened and that there should be *some* kind of independent China. For another, the ultimate prize—and he believed that Chiang Kai-shek could be "squeezed like a lemon to the last drop and then thrown away"— was obviously the whole country. His quandary may be measured by the fact that at one level he was playing safe and at another double-or-nothing.

It was Chiang, in the event, who "squeezed the lemons." The standard interpretation is that his main reason for veering eastward toward Shanghai was to make a bargain with business and foreign diplomatic interests whereby he would obtain financial backing and suppress the Communists. Malraux adopts this with the simple modification that the role of intermediary, originally said to have been played by the French consul in Shanghai, is given to the big businessman Ferral, whom he presents as the president of the French chamber of commerce and a friend of the consul. At all events, Chiang arrived outside Shanghai in February 1927, waited inscrutably while a largely spontaneous workers' insurrection was brutally suppressed by the resident warlord, and only entered the city after the second, successful insurrection of March 21—with which *La Condition humaine* begins. Maneuvering with a skill which paralyzed the Communists until they fell back on the purely negative step of burying their arms, he set up a separate workers' organization and placed his men in key positions, carefully balancing each step with protestations of loyalty to Hankow. On April 12 he struck, with the lightning dawn swoop whose bloody aftermath provides Malraux with the climactic scene in which he gives concrete form to Pascal's metaphor of the human situation, and expresses his own lyrical sense of fraternity-in-death.

Would Trotsky have succeeded where Stalin failed? In retrospect, it hardly seems likely; indeed, one of the standard analyses suggests that he would have lost even sooner.[3] Stalin's information was inadequate and his timing bad. He seriously underestimated Chiang Kai-shek and he did not fully grasp the social composition of the Kuomintang. However Trotsky perhaps fell into the opposite error of seeing the interests of the bourgeoisie in backward countries as being immediately identifiable with those of world imperialism. Again, he was equally poorly informed, and he did not openly come out in favor of withdrawal from the Kuomintang until the spring of 1927, when it was in practice too late. The fact is that the battle for power in Russia between Stalin and Trotsky was itself a major reason for the failure, in that it created internal conflict and confusion within the movement in China. Add to this that the Communists were still only a tiny minority facing a formidable combination of landowners, business interests, right-wing nationalists, and foreign powers, and that the resourceful Chiang controlled the army. In taking an anti-Stalinist line Malraux was certainly right to criticize Moscow for its dogmatism, but there is more than hindsight to suggest that China at this time was not ripe for a Communist revolution.

If only for artistic reasons, however, Malraux has to suggest that it *was* ripe, and to stylize the situation in other ways. Chou En-lai, the historical counterpart of Kyo, in fact escaped and fought on elsewhere—but that was in the relative world of history. In the tragic and absolute world of "Destiny," the revolutionaries, if they are to be heroic, must die. And their death, if it is to have the necessary poetic resonance, must obviously seem inescapable. Accordingly, whereas as Chiang's former political adviser Chou would have had no illusions about the tactical jousting going on, Kyo must be taken unawares; he must, in practice, be betrayed by Moscow.

This leaves Malraux with the real problem of providing a man who *must* be defeated and who has also been surprised by events with a positive political alternative to the Moscow line, but he contrives to do so in a way which to the average reader will seem plausible enough. He lends to Kyo a kind of romantic Leninism, with the emphasis on will and on praxis rather than historical determinism, and in his treatment of his discussion at Hankow with the Comintern representative Vologuine—the liquid quality of whose name (a variant of the historical Voitinsky) goes well with his feminine plumpness, his "ecclesiastical hands," and his lack of passion except when party discipline is involved—he skillfully suggests a communism fossilized into the bureaucratic institutionalism of a dogmatic church.

However Malraux's political gloss on the situation, informed and intelligent as it is, remains on the surface; politics, in the end, is not much more than the plot. Kyo's strong plea for an immediate peasant revolution comes too late even in terms of

the novel itself, since unlike him the reader knows that Ferral
has already laid his plot with Chiang and the bankers. Again,
his own exalted feelings after the interview fall so readily and
so romantically into the larger despair informing the novel as
to suggest that "Moscow and the opposed Western capitals"
are really acting as suitably remote modern historical counter-
parts for the old gods of tragedy.

Kyo's revolutionary activity is morally cut down to size by
the parallelism of *divertissements* in the novel and, in particular,
by the obvious parallel between his own dependence on bureaucratic Moscow and that of his opponent Ferral on the effete
capitalism represented by the government in Paris. In fact, he
can make little headway in the darkly stylized world of what,
philosophically, is ultimately an antirevolutionary novel. What
is the revolutionary force of a fraternity which is to be achieved
only in defeat and in death? What can be the political force
of a view of Marxism as will rather than "fatality" in a fictional
world where Kyo's own life is suspended, and lost, on the most
ironically trivial of "fatalities": the obsession of the marginal
Dostoevskeyan clown Clappique, lingering fatefully at the
roulette table, with a perversely spinning little ball?

Politics implies acceptance of the reality of the world. The
pessimism of Malraux's Pascalian perspective and the whole
tone and structure of the novel tend to deny that reality. The
Chinese revolution and historical possibility in general are everywhere subordinated to the monolithic and, in the event, very
European idea of Destiny. The world of Chou En-lai and of
that French consul in Shanghai has become a dark and anguished
dream.

III *The Art of Destiny*

If Shanghai in 1927 has become a dark dream, it is a highly
consistent one which has all the *appearance* of historical reality.
For *La Condition humaine* is extremely skillfully contrived to
be convincing as a work of fiction.

The range of characters, some of whom are of compelling
interest, is a wide one. Among the revolutionaries there is the
engaging Russian Katow, who fulfills his life through comradeship in action; Kyo, who overcomes his vulnerability as a half-

caste through revolutionary service and through his marriage of equal partnership with his doctor wife May, though he will be driven to measure the problem of solitude by a momentary infidelity on her part; and Tchen, the terrorist disoriented by a clash of different traditions, who, once he enters the "timeless" world of murder in the brilliant opening scene, will be driven to the appalling isolation of the man who finds erotic satisfaction in murder. The world of the revolutionaries thus merges at one end into that of their opponents, whose motivation tends to resemble that of Malraux's earlier heroes. There is Ferral, a fairly straightforward if highly intelligent Fascist figure defined in terms of a drive to power and erotic domination compensating for an inner despair, whose counter-revolutionary success will ultimately gain him nothing and who will be humiliated in his turn by his wealthy mistress Valérie—a freer and more sophisticated version of the "new woman" than her pendant May. Ferral is paralleled by such as the police chief König, who suffers from impotence as a result of an early humiliation and whose brutality springs from self-hatred.

To complete the cyclical tie-up of characters, there are important linking figures such as Kyo's father Gisors, a wise and cultivated old contemplative given to opium and much preoccupied by the question of reality and illusion, and the sadly comic genius Clappique, who seeks to deny reality through the constant exercise of fantasy. Beyond this, we have a sufficient range of secondary characters to suggest the representative humanity implicit in the title. Some of the characters—notably Tchen, Clappique, Gisors, and Ferral—are very successful creations in themselves. However, Malraux's own aesthetic told him that convincing characters are the *end product* of the novelist's creative process: that their "reality" depends primarily upon the overall consistency of the "alternative world" or "coherent distortion of reality" which the writer is setting up in answer to an idea, and upon the completeness of their relation to it. He started as always from the other end, with the situation. And since he had somehow to combine the "verticality" of a metaphysical work with the "horizontals" of surface historical realism and political action, it is instructive to observe the skill with which he proceeds to "square his circle."

The situation, of course, has already been chosen as a means

of projecting the idea of Destiny, and it was entirely logical
that he should see the moment when that Destiny declares
itself—Kyo's trip to Hankow, which constitutes Part Three of
the novel—as being in some sense the still center of the work.
On either side of this journey to the Comintern oracle, which
has a symbolical and timeless quality about it, are the two
blocks or rapid, timed sequences in Shanghai: Parts One and
Two, dealing with the insurrection, as preparation; and Parts
Four, Five, and Six, up to the death of Kyo and Katow, as resolution. He then adds a final part, also removed geographically
and in time, as epilogue. In this way he obtains the broad
rhythm of alternating action and inaction necessary to his
purpose.

However, it is obviously going to be difficult to "take time off"
for philosophical discussions and long brooding passages of
metaphysical intensity in a novel about a dramatic political
situation where the reader must have the sense of the urgent
continuity of the world and of historical time. Negatively, but
extremely effectively, Malraux provides this by the brilliantly
simple device of dating and timing his scenes. He thus conditions the reader until a precisely indicated interval of four
hours, say, is accepted as four hours in the real world. By simply
stating the progress of historical time, he implicitly *incorporates*
the continuity of the real world into the totality of the work,
thus cleverly leaving himself free to dissect time into moments
of metaphysical awareness.

He can now further exploit this device in order to introduce
the overall rhythm of action and stillness into the individual
scene itself. While he opts in general for a classical style which
will provide the necessary unity of tone and carry the metaphysical message, he varies it in subtly varying degrees with
the "telegraphic" style developed in *Les Conquérants,* which
he uses both to create urgency and to give perspective in depth
by emphasizing that we are viewing the action through the
consciousness of the particular character. He can therefore
make a rapid, timed incision into the situation at the start of a
scene and then move smoothly toward the larger rhythms of
the contemplative style.

Having taken these basic decisions as to presentation, he can
continue what he calls his "musical composition" into the

thematic orchestration of symbol and image. As already noted, the Pascal image of the human situation is skillfully translated into the climactic scene of fraternity-in-death. The theme of solitude implicit in this is reinforced symbolically by such scenes as the isolation and "death" of the armored train, or that in which Tchen, supporting a chain of comrades on a rooftop in the thick of the fighting, nevertheless cannot feel at one with them. The theme of the division within the personality which determines this solitude at the primary level is of course symbolized by Kyo's failure to recognize his own voice on the trick "espionage" records. This is a simple invention on Malraux's part, since the historical revolutionaries of 1927 had neither time nor need for such frills—they kept contact by radio (and for this reason Kyo's visit to Hankow would not strictly have been necessary). But by introducing it so early, Malraux contrives to make it quite realistic *and* to establish immediate thematic control.

Destiny, solitude, illusion, and the frailty of identity can now be further brought out by a whole set of secondary devices and "doubletakes." There is the swinging lamp which gives Kyo the "two faces" which anticipate the two voices and, in general, a constant play of light and shade to emphasize the mystery of the human face and the idea of man as a mysterious "glow-worm" in a dark universe. There is the use of the mirror in relation to both Gisors and Clappique, and the mysterious and saving switch of identity through a mere change of clothes on the part of both Clappique and Hemmelrich. Destiny is of course embodied in the irony of the plot itself, but it is everywhere emphasized by ironic juxtaposition, as in the contrast between human urgency and the indifference of ticking clocks or the eternity of sky and stars. Add to this the controlled use of such "key words" as *Angst, crushed, blind, eternal, mad, dignity, suffering,* and one begins to measure the depth and complexity of Malraux's ordering of his material.

In this perspective we may perhaps see more clearly how he solves certain special problems of characterization. To begin with, each major character must ideally represent at once a distinctive *divertissement*: love, heroism, power, opium, or whatever, and an aspect of the historical situation—as Ferral represents the European grip on China, or Kyo and Vologuine the two revolutionary approaches. But of course such figures as Clappique and Gisors are quite marginal to a violent Chinese revolutionary situation. With characteristic boldness, Malraux justifies their thematic roles by giving each an important part in the plot itself; indeed he overplayed his hand with Clappique and finally had to cut one of his scenes. It was in fact natural that he should have done so. Since the unity of the work depends ultimately upon the characters sharing the same "metapsychology" of "living-toward-death" and Destiny, he had to exploit his comic contrast to the limit in order to give the impression of greater psychological variety than can actually exist in the novel.

Having thus made his characters as broadly equal as the situation will permit, he must now solve two further problems. While he cannot afford to particularize them too much in external terms, since they must be seen from the inside as parallel destinies, he must nevertheless adequately distinguish them, numerous as they are, from one another. Accordingly, he distances them by such economical means as giving them distinctive mannerisms of speech, or by dispatching the physical description of the secondary characters in particular through a summary comparison with animals or birds—a device which largely succeeds since he is also using animal imagery throughout in order to convey a disquieting sense of the fragility of human identity.

The other problem is that of maintaining his parallelism of destinies in the face of the tendency of the reader, approaching the work as a political novel, to think too easily in terms of right and wrong. By showing us the "bad" characters from the inside and in a certain metaphysical perspective he already tends to obviate this, of course. Even so, he makes a point of telling us, for example, that Gisors does not find it unnatural to be sitting over a drink with the man who will be largely responsible for his son's death, Ferral, and significantly, whereas Malraux knew that hired thugs as well as mercenary troops had been involved in the repression, he is careful to present the Kuomintang soldier advancing with bare bayonet toward Hemmelrich as acting in the name of a faith and not for money. In a word, he is at some pains to prevent moral and political considerations from interfering with the equality of metaphysical plights demanded by the overall conception.

The irony of this elaborate "Pascalian" construction— which shows what a far cry the deliberate artistry of the "dominated writer" is from on-the-spot heroic *reportage*—is that Malraux succeeded in presenting revolutionary heroism as just one human possibility among others only too successfully. Upon reading his first draft, he felt that it was altogether too black. And it was in fact as an afterthought that he added the famous episode in which Katow gives his cyanide pill to his two frightened young comrades and thus, symbolically, so dominates his "living-toward-death" as to be able freely, if very paradoxically, to go one better than the earlier Perken by "giving away" his death. Malraux could thus hope—for all the old contradiction between his metaphysical pessimism and his temperamental activism—that the intensity of the death scenes could serve at least as a poetic answer to the irony, loneliness, suffering, defeat, and death everywhere emphasized by his approach.

It is upon this delicately tenuous balance, and upon this desperate paradox, that the positive values of *La Condition humaine*: dignity and fraternity, ultimately depend.

IV *The Ambiguities of the Heroic Stance*

While *La Condition humaine* is a brilliantly executed novel, and compelling as one reads it, its dark ambiguities tend to linger on in the mind until they resolve themselves finally in other terms.

Malraux's idea of Destiny, like Pascal's image of the human situation, may possess something of the dark truth of the X-ray photograph. The trouble with the X-ray plate, however, is that it tends to dispense with certain intermediates which in life are normally experienced as realities: it may not indicate whether a man is happy, or in love, or even whether he is alive or dead. Pascal's enterprise in hollowing out the world is at least a coherent one, since the negative itself is a kind of argument for the positive of the possibility of God. Malraux, on the other hand, falls at once into an extraordinary sort of paralysis in which he feels for the suffering of the Chinese workers but can only see the revolution as an occasion or backcloth, in which he believes in action but can only see it in a perspective which tends to deny its moral content—in which, in a word, he is trying to argue for Will over Fatality within an overall structure arguing for Fatality over Will.

At the heart of this paralysis is his continuing obsession with death. The hero may now die for a cause and thus lend some historical meaning to his life, but the contradiction which had dictated the hysteria underlying Perken's deluded attempt to personalize death is still present. For the Pascalian perspective inevitably maintains the Heideggerian idea of "living-toward-death" which—by confusing finitude with mortality, defining life in terms of the "only reality" of death and, indeed, seeing "authentic" living as consisting in the "constant expectation" of death—tends to turn life inside out.

It is after all not death which governs our finitude. If for the simple reason that we can only be one person in one place at one time, we should be finite even if we were immortal. Nor, since death is an external contingency over which we have no control, can it be "incorporated" as the mainspring of being. Outside the quite exceptional situation of a man condemned to death at a particular time, the earnest "expectation" of death is a form of earnest self-deception; one might, as it were, be so resolutely preoccupied with facing up to one's mortality as to allow oneself to get mortally run over in the street. This negative and "inside-out" definition of life may poison it by falsifying experience at its source. Malraux tends to create an overall atmosphere in which the *necessary* final ontological solitude of the individual—he would hardly be an individual if he did not possess it—not only cannot find relief in ordinary social forms but is turned into an anguish bordering on panic.

So it is that the individual, basically, is seen as mad; nothing is real. "Every man is mad," says Gisors, echoing Kyo's feeling that, for himself, he is a kind of mad self-assertion. Separated both from himself and from others, the individual is a little world of suffering and solitude surrounded by blackness. He cannot, not even in the moving relationship between Kyo and May, achieve any real communication with others since in the end, as Gisors says, it is impossible to know other people. At best he can try to *colonize* other people, and even then he will be communicating only with himself. Accordingly, from a sick,

dark, panic-stricken world thrown open by the collapse of all
connection to the saturating sense of death, he stretches out
toward some absolute. This yearning takes three related forms
in the novel: death, communion with others, and godhead;
"every man dreams of being God," says Gisors, while Kyo himself feels the *Angst* of "being no more than a man." Yet if these
three fundamental aspirations underlying the variety of *divertissements* are in practice necessarily related, it is death—since
this alone is fully attainable—which is the kingpin. Godhead can
only be attained in the form of glory and, like communion, only
through death. A world paralyzed by the obsession with death
is likely to find its resolution in death. Indeed there must be
a temptation, in Nietzsche's phrase, to "make a feast of death."

It is in this perspective that the heroic death scenes of Kyo
and Katow became very disturbing. For they do not so much
state the reality of the lives that have been lived as *define them
retroactively* in terms of the absolute of death; note the tense in
Kyo's final meditation: not "he had fought," but "he would have
fought. . . ." Death, as the *Nuova Antologia* appeared to be suggesting, is being used as the mirror of meaning. Yet a fraternity
which can only be achieved through the desperately negative
parallelism of men stripped of their normal individuality under
the pressure of torture and death is an illusory one, as the ambiguity of these scenes tends to confirm. Indeed, this is about
the only point in the novel where there is real uncertainty in
the writing.

Kyo exalts the "absolute friendship which only death can
provide" when he sees the wounded Katow lying beside him,
but does not appear to think of saying goodbye to him before
he crushes the cyanide between his teeth "as though giving an
order"; his death is essentially an act of self-affirmation. Even in
the striking gesture of Katow there is in the end more affirma-
tion than denial of self. Proceeding from a feeling not of fraternity but of loneliness, it is a desperate *demonstration* that he
is greater than his own solitude. And there is something almost
tragically comic about the pride which dictates his furious reaction when one of the young comrades drops the cyanide ("to
have given *that* only for this idiot to drop it!"), as about the
"deep joy" with which he tells the officer what he has done.

Pathetically, but disturbingly, what we seem to have in these pages is not so much a real *experience* of togetherness, as a contrived situation in which the simple fact of dying together is used to justify the *idea* of fraternity. The despair underlying the novel is such that the heroic death begins to look like the only way of making an *honorable* escape from the nightmare; the only way of fusing the impossible aspirations to death, communion, and godhead; the only way of buying from the world some sense of oneness with oneself, a little metaphysical dignity, a little historical meaning. To quote from Kyo's final thoughts: "It is easy to die when one is not dying alone. Of a death saturated by this fraternal, tremulous murmuring on all sides, in this assembly of defeated men wherein multitudes would recognise their martyrs, this bloody legend of the kind of which golden legends are made!"

Given the European context in which this famous novel appeared, there is something deeply disquieting about a novel dealing with social revolution affecting many millions of people which throws into poetic relief a desperate heroism of fraternity-in-death, and the view of human love represented by Kyo's discovery that "to accept to take with oneself into death the person one loves is perhaps the complete and unsurpassable form of love."

Malraux, however, for all his intelligence and talent, was in terms of personal development still rather young. He will go beyond this stage. And he will do so, ironically but quite logically, when he comes to grips with the dark *reality* of the Europe of the 1930s—and actually encounters death.

CHAPTER 5

The Anti-Fascist

I   Toward "Quality" and "Fraternity"

MALRAUX celebrated his Goncourt Prize by flying over the Yemen desert with his pilot friend Captain Corniglion-Molinier in search of the legendary capital of the Queen of Sheba. Romantically impractical "man of action" as he was at this time, he had long cherished the idea of exploring the desert alone à la Lawrence, disguised as a Persian. Fortunately for himself and for French literature, Corniglion-Molinier dissuaded him. For one thing, as he pointed out, the "savage Bedouins" were quite as averse to Persians as they were to Parisians, and for another, as he was to discover, Malraux's confident approach to the locals in their own tongue elicited only "astonishment and total incomprehension from Arab porter and learned sage alike."[1] The ten-hour return flight from Djibouti produced as many articles and some rather imprecise aerial photographs in L'Intransigeant — as well as some pretty colorful comment from more earthbound and traditional archaeologists. For Malraux, it was largely a romantic adventure enabling him to invoke not only Destiny and Death but also, since the wild Yemenite warriors were said to castrate their captives, that other Dark Fate which is rumored to be even Worse.

Within a few months, however, he was at the First Congress of Soviet Writers in Moscow and beginning to "assume his responsibilities," as he puts it, to the point of becoming one of Europe's leading anti-Fascist writers. Over these next few years from 1934 onward, we find him active in the Association of Revolutionary Writers and Artists; delivering frequent speeches on politics and art; becoming a founder-member of the International Writer's Association for the Defense of Culture; going to Berlin with André Gide to present an appeal for the liberation of the Bulgarian Communist leader Dimitrov; speaking in London, Madrid, Moscow, and New York, and also, of course, fighting on the Republican government side in the Spanish Civil War. As the political situation in Europe after Hitler's rise to power and with the collapse of the League of Nations over Ethiopia became painfully clear, as Left and Right became more sharply polarized, and as the Comintern and the French Communist party moved from pure opposition toward the broad alliance that found its expression in Blum's Popular Front, Malraux found himself in the thick of the fight against fascism in Europe.

What lay behind his activity at this time? There was, of course, that temperamental nervous activism which led him to tell his wife in 1936 that since she had left him he had been able to *act* much more. But there were also his intelligence and his culture which could not accept the obscurantism of a Fascist ideology; his attack on this "barbarism which sacrifices men to myths," as on those conservative and Catholic writers who were prepared in the name of "Latin civilization" to condone Mussolini's attack on Ethiopia, is closely argued and precise. There was his sense of his own situation as a novelist, his view that the writer is one "entrusted with maintaining human dignity." There was the will to pursue, without abandoning his tragic view of the situation of the individual, the struggle underlying his own writing to establish that dignity. Above all, and governing all perhaps, as the strong emotional response in his speeches to experiences of dignified solidarity suggests, there was the longing of this rather solitary man for the high communion among men which he had so far only woven pathetically into his fictional representation of suffering and death. Malraux's anti-fascist activity was part and parcel of a personal struggle toward universality.

It also, of course, depended upon a reading of the overall European situation. Even before the outbreak in Spain led him to believe that "the first world civil war had begun," he felt that the weakness of the democracies in the face of the rising strength of fascism was such that the real struggle for power in greater Europe lay between fascism and communism and that, whether he liked it or not, the intellectual wishing to retain the cultural values of liberal democratic society must take account of this. Malraux himself, who is fond of saying that in politics it is important to choose one's enemy, did not so much opt for

communism as opt *against* fascism and, not being by temperament a "non-interventionist," he intervened. However, while he
accepted the presence of the Communists in a broad alliance
and tended like so many others—at least until the purges set in—
to take an open and hopeful view of the human possibilities of
the new Soviet society, he is not to be seen as having been either
a Communist or a "Communist dupe."

His, in fact, is not a case of "the God that failed." The psychology of art which he was already elaborating in fragmentary
form during these years was recognized as being non-Marxist,
while in Moscow in 1934 he wrote off as "photography" the
work of Soviet writers operating—through "a misunderstanding
about the nature of culture"—in terms of Socialist Realism. He
consistently rejected class definitions of art and the application
of doctrine to literature, and went on presenting the artist as
one "working essentially to create his own myth." Though he
later had a brush with Trotsky over the issue of the immediate
collectivization of the land in Spain, which he rejected as a policy,
he protested strongly in 1935 against Trotsky's expulsion from
France and deprecated the silence of the French Communist
party on this occasion as rather pathetic and shameful. Nor
did the Communists regard him as one of themselves. Such
fellow writers as Aragon treated him, not without mistrust, as
being merely a sympathetic outsider. Malraux, through these
demanding years, remained his own man and the tragic, faintly
aristocratic idealism of "quality" and "virile fraternity" giving
consistency to his speeches and writings at this time remains
firmly within his own line of development.

What happened was rather that the new international solidarity
of the opposition to Hitlerism provided him with an *ethical*
climate in which he could carry one stage further his myth of
"Man." He does not abandon his early analysis of European
civilization, and even develops in theoretical terms his view of
the tragic dichotomy within the individual caused by the difficulty
of reconciling the "inner consciousness" and the "outer consciousness." However, his rereading of Aeschylus has led him
to see a triumph in tragedy itself: the artist contains destiny
by the simple fact of representing it just as human civilizations,
even if man's existence on the planet remains a dark and grievous
mystery, have tamed the forces of nature and contained death

through ritual. The trouble is that whereas previous civilizations
tied the individual systematically to the world and to the cosmos
in such a way as to give him a clear ontological status—as the
Christian idea of the soul gave him an absolute "quality," and
ultimate equality—European Man is now lost and divided. For
"the West has invented the civilization of quantity as against
the world which had known only civilizations of quality, and
our task is now to give men quality." Even if man, with the
collapse of religion, has lost his soul, he must try to achieve some
equivalent awareness of his own final dignity, or "quality."

This, for Malraux, implies an acceptance of the idea of universal brotherhood, a climate of fraternity. But it is a "virile
fraternity." What makes his tragic humanism a heroic one is
that it places this fraternity above mere social fellowship. It
is still on the basis of suffering and incompleteness, and on the
"authentic" *recognition* of these, that dignity or "quality" has
to be established. Ordinary social forms cannot give this status
to Man, any more than can a social or historical determinism,
or the prevalent vague individualism which he still sees as
leading away from the universal toward an arbitrary particularity.
The myth is rather of a number of "authentic" individuals overcoming their incompleteness and participating in "Man" by
banding together in the active defense of the idea of human
"quality." It amounts to an interim and still somewhat aristocratic kind of secular religion. If it is largely dependent upon
the particular historical moment, and upon the existence of an
easily identifiable enemy of "Man" to enforce the heroism, it at
least enables Malraux to move toward seeing Destiny, no longer
in totally pessimistic terms, but in terms of possibility.

The first enactment of this myth of Promethean and "fundamental" man is in *Le Temps du mépris*.

II   Le Temps du mépris

This short work is more of a *nouvelle* than a novel, and its
plot is a simple, unilinear one. The place is Hitler's new Germany.

Having taken the calculated risk of walking into a Nazi trap in
order to seize the opportunity of destroying a list which would
incriminate the members of a clandestine network, Kassner, a
Communist writer with a "legend" who has been playing an im-

portant role as an important underground organizer, is captured and questioned. Since his identity cannot immediately be established from an old photograph, he is thrown into a stone cell, beaten and kicked into insensibility by dimly apprehended guards, and left to rot over a period of eight days.

Losing his sense of time and fearing the onset of madness— since he must retain enough self-control not to give away others under further interrogation or torture—he attempts by remembering music to order the fantasies assailing him, notably the nightmarish vision of a vulture tearing at his flesh and threatening the very center of his identity: his eyes. Ultimately, however, the music fails him, and he is driven to a sense of defeat made the more complete by the knowledge that he has no way even of committing suicide. What saves him is a comradely message tapped through the wall from a neighboring cell which, even though it is brutally interrupted by unseen guards, gives him the courage to go on in exalted and almost conquering fashion to prepare a long, imaginary speech on the theme of fraternity within the revolution. On the ninth day, as in a dream, he is led from the cell, and released. Another prisoner, probably dead from torture by now, has declared himself to be Kassner. A party contact risks his life to fly him through an appalling storm over the mountains to Prague where, after searching for her at a political rally, he is finally reunited with his wife.

It might at first seem that the climate of Malraux's work has not basically changed. The theme is still that of man struggling with his destiny in the face of suffering and death. We still have the darkness, the claustrophobia, the shadows like great spiders on the walls, the fear of madness, the constant, telling images of blindness. The prison is perhaps the central symbol in Malraux's writings, and Kassner is confined at once within a prison with walls and the prison of the self. Again, he never knows who painfully taps the message from the neighboring cell, never knows who it is who has declared himself to be the "real" Kassner, or why. And for all his miraculous escape he knows it is only a matter of time before he is captured again, to be tortured and killed: that there is no cheating his fate in the end.

Nevertheless, Kassner is defined in terms of his relation to a human community and a collective purpose rather than in terms of a fundamental *Angst*, and his solitude and "madness" in his cell are felt to be imposed by special circumstance. And Malraux develops the new open-ended version of his myth in clear ascending stages. Alone in his cell, Kassner is saved not by music, which tends in Malraux to symbolize simple happiness, but by the anonymous, grim solidarity of his unseen comrade. Together in the storm with the courageous pilot whom he barely knows—and does not *need* to know, since he knows the essential— he experiences the force of fraternal defiance of the "cosmic fury." Finally, in the multitude at the rally in Prague, he finds again "the passions and the truths which are given only to men assembled." If the happiness of his reunion with his wife is darkened by the knowledge that he must soon go off again, Malraux is trying to suggest that it is also given depth by their acceptance that happiness is interdependent with a respect for human freedom, which Kassner has already felt to be man's "awareness of, and *organization* of the fatalities bearing upon him." The emphasis has shifted from fraternity-in-death toward a fraternity beyond death, toward "the eternity of the living and not the eternity of the dead."

When Roger Stéphane suggested to Malraux in 1945 that the Communists tended to prefer *Le Temps du mépris* to his other novels, he replied characteristically: "What do you expect? It's a dud."[2] While I agree that the work is not altogether convinc- ing, I think that it is inaccurate to ascribe this to any intention to write propaganda. It is true that the novel may look like a circumstantial piece, a tribute to such German writers as Ludwig Renn, imprisoned at this time for "literary high treason." How- ever, it is significant that, whereas Renn had in fact been a Communist since 1928 and had declared at his trial that he would belong to the party until he died, Malraux—unconsciously assimi- lating his case to his own—presents him in a speech of 1935 as an intellectual who did not see the future in communism but who wanted to defend the ideals of "dignity" and "virile fra- ternity." The trouble is of a different order and the failure, relative as it is, is an artistic one.

Essentially, he was attempting a rather ambitious prose poem, a modern version of *Prometheus Bound*. Had he written it as a straightforward allegory it might well have been entirely success- ful in a different way, but by combining it with a contemporary historical situation of immediate interest to the reader he is in

effect inviting him to approach it as *realistic* fiction. Thus the
fable may require that the guards beating Kassner be seen only
as shadowy entities, or that Kassner should have to contend with
the vulture and other fantasies of the "mad" inner self, but the
reader approaching it as a realistic political story may feel that
the human oppositions are not fully treated, or that Kassner
falls to pieces too quickly. The fable and the story, in fact, are
not perfectly fused. One reason is simply that Malraux as a
novelist depends heavily for his effects upon a certain urgency
of time and of action, whereas he has to cope here with a rather
static and timeless situation. To compensate, he tends to write
in too high a key, and the fantasy sequences in particular—if only
because the reader, once he has glimpsed the principle involved,
tends to be impatient with the detail—seem overwritten to the
point of being reminiscent of his early "Cubist" pieces.

However, there is another and deeper reason underlying this
relative failure at the level of concrete representation, which
one simple example may serve to illustrate. When Kassner is
freed, he feels suddenly that his wife is very lucky, as though it
were she who had escaped and not he, and the Malraux reader
may feel that the individual is at last escaping from the prison
of his own private situation. Yet when Kassner experiences the
same feeling on two further occasions, Malraux each time re-
capitulates the information and reminds us obtrusively of the
previous occasions. Here, as in the fantasy sequences, there is
a sense of strain: as though he had got his myth in place but was
not yet able to realize it with convincing naturalness in concrete
human terms. And indeed a glance at such a book as Julius
Fučík's *Notes from the Gallows*, though direct comparison with
an autobiographical account would, of course, be unfair, reveals
his difficulty at once. Though he struggles with his theme from
beginning to end, Malraux did not as yet possess the maturity
of experience necessary for a convincing representation of
communion among men.

However, he was soon to acquire it.

III   *Malraux and Spain*

He had spent some time in Spain earlier in 1936, and when
the Franquist rebellion broke out on July 18 he at once went

to Madrid. Within a few days he was back in Paris—where political circles were already deeply divided over the issue of intervention—negotiating the purchase of airplanes and other war material on behalf of the Spanish Republican government. Upon his return to Madrid, he organized and became the titular, though not, of course, the technical head of the international air squadron known as the Escadre España, which initially included mercenary pilots as well as volunteers from many countries. The story of the squadron was one of a constant effort to patch up inadequate and outdated equipment in order to meet the challenge of modern Italian and German aircraft, but it made an important military contribution at Medellin in August 1936, and was active at the battles of the Jarama and Guadalajara early in 1937. Malraux himself flew as a bombardier-gunner on sixty-five missions, and was wounded.

In March 1937, by which time the squadron had been superseded as the war became more professionalized, he toured the United States and Canada to expound the Loyalist cause and raise funds for medical supplies. Although he was prominent at an international congress of pro-Republican writers held in Madrid in July, he was above all occupied at this time with his novel *L'Espoir,* which was published by Gallimard at the end of the year. In 1938 he was again in Spain, making a film of part of his novel under great difficulties. The film version of *L'Espoir,* which is reminiscent in style of Eisenstein or Piscator, was awarded the Louis Delluc prize and remains something of a minor classic of the cinema of the period.

It is almost as though the world came one day to look like a Malraux novel, and Malraux himself went to see—but found the world different. The Spanish Civil War, which he treats in *L'Espoir* as the dress rehearsal for World War II, was an event of enormous moral and symbolical importance for his whole generation, and his is far and away the most significant piece of literature which it produced. But one reason for this is that, while he handles this grim and tragic episode with due sobriety and intelligence, he also displays a range of sympathy, a wit, a humor, a human balance which are quite new in his work; for the first time, the daylight seems to flood into this dark fictional universe. Paradoxically enough, the climate of civil war, with its experience of comradeship, *relaxed* Malraux. And his expression at this time attains a simplicity not to be found in his public utterances before or afterward.

Armand Petitjean, at a pro-Loyalist rally in Paris early in 1937, found his hostility and irony melting before this new Malraux, "marvellously simple, at ease, down-to-earth" on the rostrum: "I must admit that it was magnificent. Never in my life have I seen such self-mastery, such power of a man, of *homo loquens,* of the man himself over other men. Malraux, I did not like you overmuch, but when you spoke, not for us in the hall but for those in the trenches, you gave us some idea of human greatness. And the proof is that it was not you we were applauding, but Spain."[3]

This time Malraux really was the "witness." In Spain, and in *L'Espoir,* the legend finally came true.

CHAPTER 6

Brotherhood–and Beyond: L'Espoir

I History and Art

FOR Malraux himself, as for many of his admirers, *L'Espoir* remains his greatest achievement. However, certain of his critics have been embarrassed by what they have felt to be journalistic or propagandist elements in the novel, and have sometimes drawn rather purist distinctions between art and history, as between art and moral or political commitment. Yet the novel has never been a highly specific or "autonomous" form, it has frequently treated historical or political conflict, and it has certainly never excluded a moral viewpoint on the part of the author; some of the arguments advanced against *L'Espoir*, indeed, could be used against most of the great nineteenth-century novelists. This approach seems to me to spring in the main from a political misreading of the novel, and perhaps also— since these critics often find nothing particularly "journalistic" about *Les Conquérants*, or "propagandist" about Malraux's preference for the Chinese revolutionaries as against Chiang Kai-shek in *La Condition humaine*—from the fact that the issue is on this occasion nearer home and to some extent still morally alive.

Malraux, in fact, was too ambitious a writer and had too high a view of himself as an artist to wish to write propaganda. He wished rather to pursue the attempt to establish his own myth of "quality" and "fraternity" and, since the acid test of a myth of this kind is its applicability to historical reality, the Spanish Civil War offered a peculiar challenge: a field of application at once promising and daunting. That he was focusing on one side in a historical conflict would not in itself have troubled him. Many great writers before him had done so, if only for reasons of manageability and clarity of viewpoint, and had still achieved universality to the extent that their work depended, not upon political particulars, but upon human values large enough to be inclusive of the other side. Malraux could not believe that his own universals of justice, brotherhood and human quality were inadequate, and he could in fact see beyond the battle to the tragedy of human strife itself.

However, there were special problems to the writing of *L'Espoir,* of course, and he was aware of them.

The first problem, which has some bearing on the charge that he was using "journalistic" material, was that he was writing about a violently contentious and highly symbolical historical conflict while it was actually going on. In practice, this meant that he could only impose his myth insofar as he was seen to respect the sheer size and diversity of a most complex situation—and insofar as he nevertheless imposed artistic unity upon his presentation of these first nine months of the war up to March 1937. Now at the simple documentary level *L'Espoir* is still to be regarded as one of the most valuable accounts of the war. But the novel could only reasonably be called "journalistic" either if it were badly written, whereas it is generally brilliantly written, or if the historical detail were gratuitous in the sense that it was not subordinated to the overall artistic purpose. Yet Malraux surely maintains an almost astonishing thematic and artistic control over his material in *L'Espoir.* Nor is it reasonable, for example, to suggest that his account of the bombing of Madrid "dates" in that there was much more elaborate bombing of civilians in World War II. What then should we say of the historical content of the novels of Balzac or Tolstoy?

The second problem was of a moral and political kind. Those critics who see a propagandist intention in the work tend curiously to take Malraux's own distinction between "being" and "doing"—between the high aspirations informing a cause on the one hand, and the discipline, energy, and compromises needed to win a war on the other—in order to suggest that politically he falls clearly on the side of the latter. The irony of this is that it seems to get Malraux's own problem upside down. He himself, in almost obsessional fashion, sees the opposition between "being" and "doing" as a tragic one, and this tragedy is in the thematic sense the very subject of the novel. It is represented and debated, often in anguished terms, from beginning to end and Malraux, not being a propagandist, does not conclude. He was not after all dealing with some sort of private moral distinction, but with

one of the great hard acts of historical life: that men fighting in
the name of freedom may have to accept the hierarchized discipline of an army, may consider it necessary to bomb Dresden
or obliterate Nagasaki—with the fact that, as one of his spokes-
men says in the novel, there may be just causes but war itself
can never be just. And by March 1937, that fact was already
making itself felt in Spain.

To begin with, there was the simple human cost of the war.
With the new techniques of *Blitzkrieg* and the attack by German
bombers on the civilian population of Madrid, war, from being
a stylized set piece, was for the first time in history becoming
total war. And this in itself imposed a new logic upon the pursuit
of the Republican cause. The battle of Madrid saw a large but
confused and ill-equipped urban population under heavy attack
by a quite small but highly equipped and disciplined professional
Franquist army consisting mainly of Moorish troops and legion-
aries. The hard lesson was obviously that the rather disparate
groupings defending the government—Socialists, Anarchists, liberal Catholics, and republicans—must meet this challenge with a
comparable degree of military organization, or be defeated.

Yet some of these elements, particularly the large Anarchist
group which in some sense represented the romantic "soul" of
opposition to the old order in Spain, could not temperamentally
or philosophically adapt easily to meet this challenge. Again,
the necessary equipment and military advice to match the assistance given to France by the Fascist countries came in the
end rather from Soviet Russia than from the "noninterventionist"
liberal democracies. In these circumstances, the highly disciplined Communist minority came to have a disproportionately
strong influence both in the army and in the administration. In
fact, this general shift from the early, heady Republican fraternity
toward a recognition of the grim necessities of modern war, and
toward the increasing relevance of the organizational merits of
the Communists, was not a private interpretation or "political
line" on Malraux's part. It was rather part and parcel of the
historical reality in terms of which this non-Communist writer—
who, incidentally, had more than one brush with the party in
Spain—had to try to establish his myth of "quality" and "fraternity."

In seeking to turn immediate history into art without simplifying abusively or descending to propaganda, therefore, Malraux was not only taking on a formidable descriptive and intellectual task. Given the passions which the war aroused, he was setting out to walk a tightrope. My own feeling is that, apart from minor uncertainties in the portrait of the character Manuel, he hardly ever, in the course of this very long novel tossed off in eight months, looks like putting a foot wrong. Richly human and glittering with talent as it is, this is surely one of the great political novels of the century. What is striking about the book, and what justifies its frequent lyricism, is the way in which it combines emotional involvement and analytical intelligence with an extraordinary detachment; almost every major character is not only troubled by the problem of ends and means but is stopped in his tracks, at one moment or another, by a sharp sense of the smallness and apparent gratuitousness of all human effort in the light of the indifference of the physical world and of eternity. "There is in this book," wrote Ramon Fernandez, "a desire to win and yet a subtle dislike of winning which for me constitutes its principal beauty."[1] It is a measure of the literary distinction of the novel that it establishes the war in Spain not just as a battle or a political equation, but as a poignant human mystery.

It is interesting that so many critics, even among those opposed to Malraux politically, should have recognized the nature of the achievement when the work first appeared. That he does not distort the Franquists as human beings was attested by Jacques Madaule and others. That his picture of the Republican side is less than idyllic emerges eloquently enough from the backhanded compliment of the Fascist writer Robert Brasillach who, after suggesting that the novel was likely to do more harm than good to morale, adds: "In fact, I know of no pamphlet more damaging to the cause of the Revolution."[2] Finally, that there is genuine psychological and moral conflict in the novel was obvious from almost every page. "Of all the books which have appeared in the last twenty years," wrote Montherlant, hardly a political bedfellow of Malraux's, "this is the one which one would most like to have lived and written."[3]

To compare the merits of *La Condition humaine* and *L'Espoir* is not easy. If the former is more completely polished as art, this is perhaps balanced by the sweep, the color, and the descriptive

energy of the latter. Again, the novels are not so much different
in kind as written in different keys. Malraux's basic themes are
still present in *L'Espoir*. Not only does he smuggle in his Gisors-
like old art historian Alvear to give the final edge of irony and
ambiguity to the title, but he repeats the symbol of Kyo's record
in the shape of the initial grievous inability of a peasant, taken
up in an airplane to point out a camouflaged Franquist airfield,
to recognize the little patch of earth where he has lived and
labored all his life. There is the same metaphysical perspective,
and ambiguity, in each. Yet there is one important difference
which might seem to justify Malraux's own preference for
L'Espoir.

In *La Condition humaine* the ambiguity, in that it is partly
a function of self-contradiction in Malraux's own world view,
is felt to some extent to be superimposed upon the historical
world. In *L'Espoir,* which was the product of a unique balance
between the writer's vision and a fully resistant, because fully
apprehended reality, the ambiguity is felt rather as the tragic
complexity and confusion of the world itself. In *La Condition
humaine* the characters seemed to suffer in a dark and stylized
night; in *L'Espoir,* they suffer in the hard Spanish daylight.

And Malraux had the painterly eye required to render it.

II *Toward the Epic Vision*

The first general impression one receives from *L'Espoir* is that
Malraux has found a subject which has in some sense set him
free: at once broadened his range of awareness and sympathy
and unleashed the whole range of his literary skills. And one
seems to sense also that this derives from a new experience of
the world and of "fraternity." In *La Condition humaine* fraternity
was a desperate aspiration, to be consummated in death.   In
L'Espoir, from Gonzalez's "hard and fraternal exaltation" in the
face of the oncoming tanks, or the excellent battle scene in which
two members of an International Brigade, separated by language,
address each other in bird song, to the grandiose scene which is
perhaps the summit of Malraux's writing—the "descent from the
mountain" scene in which a whole village with profound and
almost ritual simplicity comes to the aid of wounded airmen
after a crash—fraternity, at last, is attained.

While *L'Espoir* is still a tragic novel, its mode is different from that of *La Condition humaine* in that Malraux is moving from "vertical" stylized tragedy toward a panoramic and, indeed, an epic vision. If only because in war it is an everyday reality, death is no longer a constant, nagging, metaphysical obsession. The physical world itself is no longer felt by the characters to be so oppressive or threatening; that stifling, claustrophobic quality so characteristic of many of the key scenes of the earlier novels is no longer central. The pressure of solitude, estrangement, and noncommunication is now so relaxed as to admit something of the relativity of ordinary existence. Freed from the unifying "metapsychology" of living-toward-death and Destiny, the characters seem to achieve a certain separate identity and psychological freedom: they get tired, joke, eat meals, and succeed in taking one another's existence and their own for granted.

Again, some of the characteristic attitudes of the earlier work are now crowded out. Eroticism and "mythomania" disappear, except insofar as they provide comic interludes, while a number of remarks—"there is no hero without an audience," or "the first volunteers were all more or less madmen or heroes, and sometimes both"—suggest that Malraux has now firmly taken the measure of the early adventurer-heroes. In fact, we see him moving away from rather literary, majuscularized conceptions such as Death, Destiny, and Hero toward the simple representation of men in situation. But this change in the immediate climate of his writing does not mean that the writer has lost his vision; it means rather that he is realizing it more convincingly in terms of the historical world. And the world does not become less mysterious for being more real; on the contrary, it becomes for Malraux the more mysterious.

This new freedom and this epic sweep are, of course, seen in the very structure of the novel. Part One, *L'Illusion lyrique,* which takes up about half of the work, ranges in a series of quickly alternating scenes from events surrounding the Franquist rebellion of July 18 in Madrid and in Barcelona, through the military action of the young Communist Manuel in the Sierra and the activities of Magnin's International Air Squadron outside Madrid and at Medellin, to the drama of the besieged Alcazar at Toledo and the loss of the city by the badly disorganized Republicans at the end of September—before settling on the personal tragedy of the Republican officer Hernandez. Part Two, also lengthy and named after the river Manzanares, covers the period from the start of November to early December, maintaining the interest in the Air Squadron and in the military situation of the International Brigades, but concentrating essentially on the defense of Madrid, before settling on the personal dilemma of Manuel. The much shorter Part Three, entitled *L'Espoir*, runs from February 8 to the latter part of March 1937, and includes the confused exodus from Málaga and scenes from the battles of the Jarama and Guadalajara, as well as the famous descent-from-the-mountain episode. However, this can convey only the broadest idea of the confident ease with which Malraux switches from one part of Spain to the other, and from one to another of a formidably large cast of characters.

The principle governing his technique is one of flexible juxtaposition: of locale with locale, and of action scene with meditative passage or conversation piece. He seems, one might almost say, to combine the advantages of the novel, the film and the play of ideas. Yet it is perhaps of the cinema that his art is most suggestive. His "scenes" tend to be stylized and finished units in themselves, within which he moves fluently from the panoramic to the closeup, often completing his fadeout interrogatively with a telling symbolical shot; the juxtaposition or "editing" of these scenes itself largely provides narrative perspective and continuity. His virtuosity is also seen in the skill with which he handles different levels of language, varied styles of conversation and gesture, and quite diverse types of action. Whether the immediate background is Toledo or a small village, whether he is describing a bombing raid, a tank attack, or an execution, he always seems to be able to provide the authentic detail—and the authentic oddity of incidental detail—which will establish the reality at once of the scene and of the character involved.

However, his narrative control is not simply a function of rhythm or of cinematic editing. For all the diversity of the scenes, we are concerned in the main with only two or three major centers of developing interest. And though he also contrives quite plausibly at certain moments to bring his major characters together, it is essentially in relation to their particular area of interest that he establishes each—providing each with foils and with such satellite or minor characters as need to be knitted successfully into the fabric of so ambitious and complex a work.

Thus the military aspect constantly involves the rising young Communist Manuel, with the Catholic Colonel Ximénès as foil, and such other significant figures as Heinrich. The Anarchist aspect introduces us to Puig, the Negus, and various spectacular minor figures. The aviation aspect centers upon the mustached French commander Magnin, but also involves the young Italian art historian Scali, and partly thereby the old sage Alvear. A special role is played by Garcia, anthropologist turned Intelligence chief, who is well placed to act as focus for discussion of the political and moral issues involved. Yet if Garcia is not unlike Malraux by dint of his turn of speech and formidable analytical power, Magnin—though Malraux has completely distanced him as to age and physique to obviate comparison with himself—perhaps remains closer to his creator by his deeper will to fraternity.

Beyond the structural control obtained through the exercise of this general relating principle, and quite apart from the intelligence and concern with which he isolates the central moral problem from a complex political situation, Malraux seems to possess his situation both in depth and in breadth. In depth, insofar as he can see the civil war in terms of Spanish history: the fresh ruins as a stage in a series going back to Christian, Roman, or Punic ruins. Not only has he the visual gift of rendering the Spanish light, the colors of a landscape or village rooftops, a detail of a building in Toledo or Madrid; he has the culture required to convey the agony of an Unamuno, or to set the present against the background of the country of El Greco, of Spanish Christendom, of the whole history of human effort in the peninsula. In breadth, he controls the situation by seeing it firmly in its international context. He points to the irony that Hitler's Junkers bombers were not quite the menace that the democracies had feared, or to the irony of Italian volunteers fighting Mussolini's Italians at Guadalajara. He already sees that the "Age of Fire" has begun with the bombing of Madrid, that all this is really the beginning of World War II, and that it will not be long before Japan itself "joins in the dance." He establishes the conflict as having worldwide symbolic importance.

It is by this multiple grid that Malraux orders his material

and gives his novel relevance and resonance. Yet all this is
governed by an ultimate control of a different and more fundamental kind, which everywhere informs the new richness of
imagery and symbolic reference which has often been noted
in *L'Espoir*.

Underlying the allusions to history or music or painting, the
imagery of light and shade, or sun and snow, or sound and
silence, there is again a constant principle of juxtaposition. The
opposition may be ironic or absurd, comic or tragic: a barricade
made up of confessionals, people undressed but otherwise un-
harmed by an explosion, a butterfly on a dead man's face, stuffed
bears trembling in an air raid, a battle outside a sunlit cemetery,
birds passing on their annual migration in the course of an air
action. It comes out forcefully in the references to the carnival,
the fairground, or the film set: militiamen, dressed in a style
veering grotesquely between that of the Mexican revolutionaries
and that of the Paris Communards of 1871, seen against the
up-to-date Le Corbusier buildings of the airport; or homeless
children seeking refuge beneath giant Disneyland figures during
an air raid. It everywhere expresses the new kind of ultimate
polarity which goes with the epic vision in *L'Espoir*: the constant
opposition of illusion and reality, of the moment and the infinite,
of the passionate "madness of men" and the idle indifference of
sun-drenched cemetery, or shimmering plain, or evening red
over snowy mountains.

The great paradox of *L'Espoir*, which takes it far above any
vulgar propaganda, is seen in the new "cosmic" tone informing
the meditative rhythms of the style itself. The typical ascending
movement of the sentence is from the particular, through the
collective, toward the eternal. "Everything seems to lead Malraux
to turn his eyes towards the sky," as Girard puts it, "and night
itself in *L'Espoir* seems to rise rather than fall."[4] Strangely but
logically, the very discovery of fraternity leads beyond fraternity.
The Malraux hero escapes from his dark prison of solitude and
anguish and, for the first time, sees the world beyond himself
clearly. But now that the cosmos is no longer felt as the oppressive weight of night, it comes to be felt as something more
mysterious still, and more daunting: as the ultimate indifference
of daylight.

"The sun shone brightly upon the prostrate bodies and upon

the blood": this short sentence, in the midst of a battle scene, is printed as a complete paragraph. The very reality of fraternity makes the human adventure seem stranger than ever, and raises the problem of "quality" to the highest metaphysical level. In the following very typical sentence we already see Malraux moving toward the later, reflective style of *Les Noyers de l'Altenburg* and *Les Voix du silence*: "Turning like some tiny planet lost amid the indifferent gravitation of astral bodies, the airplane waited for Toledo to pass beneath it, with its rebellious Alcazar and its besiegers alike swept along in the absurd rhythm of earthly things."

Malraux, on the ground, has discovered the reality of fraternity. Malraux, in his airplane, has risen far above the battle and discovered what he calls "geological indifference," or "geological serenity."

III   *The Ethical Problem*

Malraux's opposition between "being" and "doing"—*Être et faire* is the title of the first of the two sections in Part Two—has sometimes been taken as indicative that there are only two basic attitudes in the novel, and that he himself hovers uneasily between them. The truth is far from being so simple. There are, in fact, four basic attitudes in the novel and it is from the interplay between them, as well as from the formal or poetic persuasion of the work, that the final balance and meaning emerge.

At the immediate level, *être et faire* translates the broad opposition between Anarchists and Communists. As Garcia sees it, the Communists want to make something, whereas the Anarchists and such simply generous men as the officer Hernandez want to *be* something. The drama of their revolutionary situation is that they have to live according to conflicting myths: pacifism *versus* self-defense, the need to organize *versus* the Christian virtue of meekness, effectiveness in war *versus* justice. "We have to bring some order into these myths and transform our Apocalypse into an army, or die," he says. "There are no two ways about it."

The beginning of the war is the heyday of the Anarchists, the new dawn which Malraux, though he was temperamentally far closer to the Anarchists than to the Communists, calls the

"lyrical illusion." Men who feel that they have been oppressed
and humiliated for centuries, and with a romantic history of
defeats behind them, come face to face with this sudden, miraculous "carnival of freedom" and want to see their individualist
ethic realized at once: "to live," as the Negus declares, "as life
ought to be lived, here and now, or die." The trouble, in Garcia's
view, is that since this is not a peasant uprising but war against
a mechanized modern army, their living may indeed turn out to
be dying—and that these "semi-Christians," with their romantic
taste for self-sacrifice, may settle for martyrdom all too easily.
Like Puig, indeed, in an early scene, they tend to die heroically,
but too soon. In their will to brotherhood and freedom and a
certain personal nobility, they may incarnate for Garcia or for
Malraux the deepest impulse underlying the cause, but it is not
they who have the discipline necessary to forge the army that
achieves the holding victory with which the novel ends. It is the
Communists.

To the Communists, the Apocalypse is necessarily provisional,
an initial stage in the task of social construction. They tend
realistically to be concerned not with the absolute but with the
relative, less with nobility than with winning the war. "In the
last analysis," says Pradas, "nobility is a luxury which a society
can only afford at a late stage of development." For the Negus,
who wants "to make neither a state nor a church nor an army,
but men," the Communists have turned a cause into a party or
yet another church. He sees them as corroded by discipline and
the complicity of partisanship, while Magnin and Hernandez
also discover that the Communists will put party before individuals or justice. For Garcia, who cannot accept what he sees as
the denial of subjectivity and individuality implicit in the "objective" ethic of the Communists, they "have all the virtues of action,
and those alone—but action is what is needed at this time."

The tragic nature, for Malraux, of this broad opposition in the
initial stage of the conflict becomes clear. The Anarchists incarnate the profounder aspiration to fraternity and "quality," but
are too romantically absolutist to adjust to the challenge of
modern war. The Communists, with their rigorous relativism,
their belief in the historical process and their equal courage, can
certainly adjust to this challenge; but is there not the danger
that their tough objectivism and exclusivism, together with the

destructive nature of war itself, may drain the cause of its human meaning in the process?

Since the whole effort of the novel is to transcend the tragic dilemma implicit in *être et faire*, the center of gravity of *L'Espoir* is firmly placed outside this historical opposition between Anarchists and Communists. It is true that the logic of the developing military situation obliges Malraux to set up Manuel—who plays broadly the same role as the historical Lister, commander of the Communist Fifth Regiment—as being in a technical or formal sense the central figure of the novel. However, he possesses neither the importance nor the authority given to Garcia and he is presented, in opposition to such men as Enrique or Heinrich, as being a sensitive, intelligent young Communist who is tormented by the conflict between humanity and the cruel necessities of command. He feels that he is becoming "a little less human every day," and that "to be close to the Party is valueless if it means being separated from those for whom the Party is working." The military situation gives a certain tragic necessity to his loneliness, but his awareness of the fragility of his "terrible equilibrium" enables Malraux discreetly to "save" him from the party on the last page. Positively, therefore, as well as antithetically, he gravitates toward the group of characters who represent the third—and central—basic attitude in the novel.

Garcia, Magnin, Scali and such figures as Guernico and Ximénès, two Catholics who see themselves as fighting for Christ against both Franco and the Church of Spain, form a much more homogeneous group than might at first appear. Between them these men, non-Communist and intelligent as they are, constantly maintain Malraux's preoccupation with the quality of man, the idea of the role of the intellectual as custodian of human values, and the idea of the *difficulty* of being a man. Their political program proper is modestly stated: they want to improve the economic lot of the poor and to create a climate of justice and fellowship within which individuals may flourish freely. If the climate of fraternity is so important for them, it is because they see it as the condition of obtaining quality for the individual. They are fully aware of the opposition between "being" and "doing," or ethics and political action, but they also recognize the need to act in terms of this very reality. They are trying,

in a word, to transcend the opposition and to act in such a way
that *faire* expresses at least the direction of *être*.

In an important conversation with Scali, Garcia puts this view
very forcefully. The war, he says, is a fact. The revolution
through which they are living exists not as a solution to personal
problems but as a historical reality. They are agreed as to the
necessity of resisting fascism and are thus committed to winning
the war. Even if there is the risk that a Communist victory may
liberate the peasants economically only to enslave them politically,
as Scali suggests, they are still forced at the immediate level to
choose between the risks of action and . . . inaction. The choice
is tragic, and action necessarily unjust, but they are placed in
the midst of war and the good to which they aspire cannot be
achieved through passivity. For an intellectual to say that he
is leaving their cause because they are unjust is *immoral,* he says,
for no party can be just. There can never be more than a *policy*
of justice. That policy is theirs and it is up to them, by making
their presence felt, to see to it that quality and freedom are
maintained in Spain.

So central is this group that it is essentially among its members
that the moral debate is conducted, and indeed a certain difference between Garcia and Magnin is important in the final balance
of the novel. The three parts of the work are really three tiers
of fictional persuasion in the service of an overall "argument."
Part One presents "being" and "doing" as an *option* imposed by
the Republican confusion which leads to the loss of Toledo. The
tragedy of Hernandez, who morally commits suicide insofar
as he does not seize the chance of escaping, does not lie simply
in the world's denial of his generosity to the commander of the
Alcazar—he tells his interrogator that he might not be so generous
the next time. It lies rather in his inability to live with the hard
fact of the conflict between "being" and "doing." Part Two takes
the problem a stage further, beyond the antinomic to the cor-
relative—the title of the first section is *Être et faire,* that is *"and"*
rather than "or." Malraux indeed opens this section with several
strong scenes showing a successful combination of "being" and
"doing," emphasizing that "for the first time there was a fraternity which took the form of action." However, the graph of
this part is similar to that of the first in that we end with the
drama of Manuel, driven grievously to "choose between victory

and pity" in dealing with deserters: a drama which is none the less real for being as it were the mirror image of that of Hernandez.

The "hope" which gives the title to Part Three does not lie simply in the military success after the defense of Madrid, but in Magnin's sense that it may be possible to cope with this contradiction more successfully than Hernandez or Manuel. To reinforce this "hope," Malraux holds back in time his "descent from the mountain" scene—which had historically taken place in December—and gives it climactic poetic force. It is because he has been so deeply moved by this experience that Magnin can come to feel that Garcia is not the ultimate oracle. Garcia declares in the last scene but one that "the age of Parties" is at hand—and, as Camus and others were to verify much later, this statement was prophetic enough. Yet Magnin has witnessed the simple, fundamental solidarity of the peasants on the mountainside, and can see obscurely in this a guarantee that fraternity is a reality which must finally prevail. Even so, the conclusion remains an open-ended and fragile one insofar as these men are uncertain about the outcome and constantly uneasy about the morally damaging effect of war itself.

This leads us finally toward the fourth basic attitude in the novel, represented by the very presence of the old sage Alvear and implicit in the "cosmic tone" in the writing itself. The authority of Alvear—as Malraux's friend André Gide at once recognized[5]—lies in the fact that he states the idea of "quality" in terms of Malraux's long-standing obsession with the need for an "age of the fundamental" which will found Man and reason afresh. For him the Revolution is just another version of the old illusion of eternal life, a blind man's song of hope. His remarks linger on through the complex and delicate counterpoint through which Malraux builds up the final, mysterious meaning of his title. At the moral and political level of this moving and profoundly liberal novel he achieves a kind of positive equilibrium, but it is a difficult one, a fragile one, and a directly threatened one. And Alvear, with his reminder that there is "a deep and terrible hope in man" to which there can be no political answer, leaves it edged with black.

In the uneasy Europe of the eve of World War II, *L'Espoir* did not purvey a packaged political answer: far from it. It indicated hesitantly a difficult, if necessary moral direction, and asked some ultimate questions.

IV *Beyond* L'Espoir

Back in Paris at the start of 1939, with his novel already well behind him and with the Faubourg Saint Honoré celebrating Munich with a new line in fetishes in the shape of miniature Chamberlain umbrellas, Malraux can have held out little hope for the immediate future of "fraternity" either in Spain or throughout Europe.

At the level of personal experience, even if it had depended upon an exceptional historical situation, it had been a reality: he had achieved himself in the world as a man, and acquired a new ease and confidence. But this very fact altered his situation as a writer. No longer a haunting private aspiration or literary myth to be realized, fraternity leads beyond itself toward metaphysical speculation. Between Malraux and the "starry skies" constantly invoked in the later writings, the world no longer constitutes a powerful barrier. To the very extent that he has successfully imposed his myth upon the world, Malraux as artist no longer needs the novel—and indeed his great period of novel-writing is over. In Paris, he goes back to his psychology of art, to anthropology and the philosophy of history: to fundamentals. The stage is already set for *Les Noyers de l'Altenburg* and *Les Voix du silence*.

Yet a man cannot easily withdraw from the world or from his own life history. Malraux was overtaken by that World War II which he had so clearly foreseen, by the collapse of France and then Hitler's invasion of Russia. He had not "broken" with the Communists after the Hitler-Stalin pact, as some critics have maintained. For one thing, having pointed out early in 1937 in New York that "the first world civil war had begun," he was not entirely unprepared for the great strategic maneuvers and betrayals—this agreement or the Munich agreement—which preceded the fighting. For another thing, there was not in any very meaningful sense a "break" with the Communists to be made: Malraux was no Marxist and no Communist. However, he had been a leading anti-fascist since the rise of Hitler in Germany, he had witnessed the failure of the democracies to stop fascism,

and he now saw it rampant throughout Europe. In these circumstances, and however ironical it may seem in retrospect, his reply
to Roger Stéphane when the latter was sent by the Resistance
to invite him to come to London and join de Gaulle is not so
surprising as it might seem. "I have nothing in common with that
crowd of royalists surrounding de Gaulle," he told Stéphane.
Then, after thinking for a moment or two, he added: "If I really
did feel obliged to emigrate, my place would be with the Red
Army."[6]

CHAPTER 7

In Search of Fundamental Man (I): Spengler and Les Noyers de l'Altenburg

I The Private War with Oswald Spengler

WHEN war broke out, Malraux got himself accepted for active service and saw some fighting as a private in a tank regiment before being captured in the collapse of 1940. Sent to a prisoner-of-war camp in the cathedral town of Sens—which he was to transpose as Chartres in *Les Noyers de l'Altenburg*—he eventually escaped very much in the manner of his own Clappique in *La Condition humaine*: by putting on carpenter's overalls, throwing a plank over his shoulder, and walking out. In 1941, he assisted in one of the first significant acts of sabotage by helping to blow up a munitions train at Toulouse, but he enjoyed much creative leisure over the next two years before becoming fully active with the now highly organized underground toward the end of 1943.

Malraux's outstanding career in the Resistance, for which he was lavishly decorated by his own government as well as by the British government, need only be stated briefly here—the most interesting part of the story, his capture by the Germans in 1944, is told by himself in *Antimémoires*. It was perhaps inevitable, especially after his experience in Spain, that his temperament, his courage, and his natural authority should bring him into prominence at this time. He allied a romantic boldness of imagination with a certain hard precision of mind, and an affection for his men with a natural aloofness. In fact, as one of his admiring collaborators saw it, he combined a proud lack of personal ambition with a sort of higher dilettantism which enabled him to be at once the passionately involved leader and the ironically detached observer.[1] The *maquis* which he commanded was partly concerned in 1944 with a delaying guerrilla against the ill-famed S.S. Division *Das Reich,* then moving up

to reinforce the Normandy defenses. Wounded and captured
in an ambush, he was imprisoned in Toulouse, but delivered by
the Allied advance in the South. Incorporated into the army
with the rank of colonel, at the head of his Alsace-Lorraine
brigade under the overall command of Leclerc, he fought at the
Battle of Dannemarie and was involved in the capture of Stras-
bourg. While his basic philosophical pessimism could hardly
be dispelled by the destruction he witnessed, and while he also
suffered grievous private losses through the conflict, it is nevertheless a tough and buoyant Malraux who comes through in
interviews toward the end of the war.

For the present, however, it is the darkest moment of this
period which concerns us: the bleak year of 1941 in which Malraux wrote *Les Noyers de l'Altenburg*. If he largely turns away
from immediate history and its moral meanings in this book,
it is partly because he seems to have been too exhausted to cope
with them, but essentially because he had also reached a private
moment of reckoning. Not only did the collapse make a mock-
ery of his myth of quality-through-fraternity, but the very name
of this "Second World War" sent him back to World War I, with
which he had grown up and against the background of which he
had hacked out his stark myth of the "death of Man." As against
this, his service in the tank regiment had for the first time
brought this tense cosmopolitan intellectual into some real contact with the ordinary people of his own country. With the
greater maturity of the man approaching forty—and he seems
to have been going through a "Jungian" change at this watershed
—he had found the experience enlightening. His own sense of
self was called in question at this moment of defeat, as well as
the continuity of his career. So it is that *Les Noyers* is a kind
of return to the source: at once a postmortem and an attempt
to reconstitute a world.

There are two intimately related levels to this attempt. The
search for a fundamentality of the self necessarily goes hand in
hand, for Malraux, with a search for the fundamentality of Man.

At the first level, he is clearly trying to come to terms with
himself: with his own nature and his own legend, as well as
with his new experience of common humanity. The novel reads
almost like a private anthology in which he is projecting and
juxtaposing elements from his own life and his own writings—

transposing the suicide of his father of ten years before, or reviving the semimythical old grandfather of *La Voie royale*—in an attempt to work towards a new fusion. If it has sometimes been suggested that Malraux found a father figure in the stark, resplendent figure of de Gaulle, *Les Noyers* reminds us that major writers tend to resolve problems of this order in the projection of their own work. In this last novel of 1941, Malraux set up a parallelism of father and son, firmly played both parts as it were, and emerged with a new kind of unity. By the time he met de Gaulle at the end of the war, he was perhaps free rather to regard him as somebody more or less in his own class! Malraux is a sophisticated man, and the very ease and jocularity with which he privately referred to de Gaulle as *"le vieux"* are more suggestive of his old value of dogged loyalty to an "action" than of psychological dependence.

This search for self is of course still a mythopoeic enterprise, the examination of a fictive, projected self (which is incidentally why it was *doubly* fitting that the Malraux of the *maquis* a few years later, unable to use his own name, should have used that of the twin protagonists of *Les Noyers* to become "Colonel Berger"). One reason is simply that this is an imaginative work. Another is that Malraux, who had begun by decreeing the absurdity of the *moi* and the "death of Man," can only conceive a new awareness of self in relation to a new sense of man. Finally, Malraux was in 1941 already searching actively for the controlling conception with which he might structure what he saw as his long-delayed *summa*: his writings on the philosophy of art. The projected larger work of which *Les Noyers* is a fragment (Malraux has pointed out that his papers were seized by the Germans during the war) was to have been called *La Lutte avec l'ange*. Jacob, it will be remembered, wrestled with his unknown opponent "until the breaking of the day," and was then convinced that he had "seen God face to face." Malraux, in this agnostic "struggle with the angel" begun in the dark night of defeat, is wrestling in order to see Man face to face.

So important is this myth of "fundamental man" for Malraux from now on—he could still say in conversation many years later, with sudden, startling simplicity: "I am trying to find the reality of man, independently of (cultural) forms"—that it must be situated with some care.

To the Anglo-Saxon mind, Malraux's search for "fundamental man" may look like eccentricity or pretentiousness of quite continental proportions, even though the "fundamentality" of man is arising in different terms today as a problem for a variety of intellectual disciplines, including linguistics—there is, indeed, a certain "prestructuralist" quality about the Altenburg debate in this novel. Nevertheless, the idea of the need for a notion of "fundamental man" was obviously the axis of Malraux's work from the beginning. Arguing in his early diagnosis of Western civilization that man was "dead," after God, he suggested that civilization could only be founded afresh on a new idea of man himself: in effect, on something as firm and suprahistorical as the Christian idea of the soul. Yet this was in practice impossible in that the individual, that "monster of wish-fulfillment," could know neither himself nor others. With sciences which were mere allegories and a psychology that was mere fable, man was quite simply unknowable—and it is significant that the Vincent Berger of *Les Noyers* still maintains that psychology, far from being the analysis of *universal* man, is rather a local cultural feature: an instrumental myth of the West which has grown up in relation to the now superseded Christian view of human nature as vitiated by original sin. This initial impossibility of "being" was compounded, in the early novels, by the tragic failure of the "New Man" to smash a way out of the "metallic realm of the Absurd."

Throughout the 1930s, even if he could not provide an intellectual or existential basis for the secular religion or "tragic humanism" to which he rather desperately aspired, Malraux sought at least to establish the values appropriate to such a world view. But "dignity" in *La Condition humaine* was still negative in that it had to be "founded on suffering," and the "fraternity" a desperate paradox in that his pessimism could enable him to establish only a fraternity-in-death. In *L'Espoir*, he depicted a more real fraternity, but it was still a heroic and somewhat elitist one which was all too dependent upon the exceptional historical situation. Now that the victory of fascism has torn the bottom out of that world, he is left at once with a new experience of people and with the question posed by the ethnologist Möllberg at the Altenburg colloquy: "Is it possible to discern beneath the diversity of beliefs and myths, and above all beneath the multiplicity of mental structures, any permanent underlying element, valid for cultures everywhere and throughout history, upon which the idea of man may be based?"

The continuity of this search for the fundamental is therefore not in question. Yet in a very important sense there is a falling away. As the rather unsuccessful combination of ideas and fictional illustration in *Les Noyers* itself underlines, Malraux's great strength had lain in dramatic realization through the novel rather than in the manipulation of ideas in their own terms; romantic antirationalist as he is, he tends to treat these less as ideas proper than as myths having their own emotional field of resonance. As is so often the case, the strength of the artist is the weakness of the thinker. And now that the universality won through the flesh-and-blood immediacy of fictional projection is on the wane, the underlying intellectual thematics begin to look curiously particular, solipsistic, datable, and fragile. Malraux, indeed, might seem to be back to his beginnings with a vengeance. For the "struggle with the angel" boils down at first sight to a struggle with the now largely disregarded philosopher-historian who came to the fore in Germany after World War I with his *Decline of the West*: Oswald Spengler.

I say "at first sight" because the issue is in fact more complex than this. Even so, the key to Malraux's writings since 1941 is this struggle with Spengler. It underlies the art writings, the political speeches, and the whole expression of his "tragic humanism." He has more than once said that the first intellectual task of his generation is to refute Spengler and it was in 1952—significantly, just after the publication of *Les Voix du silence*—that he said in private conversation: "In the end, the only serious one among them is Spengler."

Now there is certainly a conflict between Malraux's aspiration to "fundamental man" and Spengler's grim vision of history as the cyclical, predictable story of different cultures compelled by the same inherent destiny, succeeding one another by the same organically inevitable process of growth and decay, and dying off irretrievably at the end of their allotted span, like individuals. In such a mechanical and meaningless phantasmagoria of irreducibly separate civilizations, there is clearly little room for fundamentality. Again, Malraux's concern with Spengler is understandable in the light of the fact that his primary intellectual interest has always been in art and archaeology; from the outset, he was confronted with the problem posed by the alien perfection of styles produced by cultures of which we know little or nothing. It should be said also that Spengler's work is in many ways interesting and suggestive. Nevertheless, there is something oddly unreal about this private war which Malraux, jumping back a generation, begins in the heart of the world war in 1941.

In the first place, if Spengler is not taken very seriously today it is not for nothing; his mechanical and in fact rather "period" application of the biological metaphor, his argumentative procedures, and his manipulation of historical facts are all open to the heaviest criticism. In the second place, Malraux, however concerned he may be that Spengler should be refuted, has never shown any inclination to do so in the intellectual terms in which it could only fully and effectively be done. Add to this the thought that Malraux's search for "fundamental man" might have been less anguished had he not so prematurely decreed that Man was "dead" in the first place, and one begins to sense that "Spengler" is shorthand for a trauma or obsession.

To some extent, of course, he symbolizes the shared "culture trauma" of Malraux's uneasy generation at the end of World War I, the "crisis of the mind" already analyzed in Chapter 2. Yet Spengler, if a spectacular one, was just one of a whole set of influences operating within the Nietzschean perspective and mediating ideas of decline and cultural discontinuity. His impact upon this largely self-educated young man, dependent to some extent at this time of travel and discovery upon Clara's German culture, was an exceptionally heavy one. Indeed, it was an intimately personal and emotional impact. For Spengler's apocalyptic thesis came almost providentially to sustain the stark myth of the "death of Man" by which Malraux objectivized and justified his own private estrangement—and upon which, after all, he based his writer's career. "Spengler," in the end, is a central part of Malraux, a code name for a deep-laid constitutive complex—at once imposed and defiantly elected— into which the quest for self of the middle years must inevitably run. Whence the often despairing lyricism of the later Malraux, and the curious impression he may leave that he is not so much refuting Spengler as trying somehow, *from within* "Spengler," to reverse his perspective.

This, then, is the problem of Malraux's last, largely non-imaginative phase. Viewed "from within," he may seem an ever richer writer bringing his long labors to high fruition in a new and noble universal humanism. Viewed "from without," he may seem a rather reduced writer engaged almost eerily—through world war, Cold War, and Gaullist politics—in a faintly manic, irrelevant dance of death with the ghost of Spengler.

II   A Poem on Man

Almost as though he were choosing it as a discipline of non-commitment, Malraux takes the quite exceptional situation of an Alsatian father and son fighting on different sides in the successive world wars, and disregards the specific political or moral problems which this obviously poses. War is now seen neutrally as a scourge which comes more or less inevitably to each generation.

Fragmented as it is, *Les Noyers* is at first sight a curiously constructed and unfinished novel. Yet even if it seems episodic it has considerable unity of atmosphere and of tone. Again, it possesses a larger if still tenuous kind of coherence in that Malraux is seeking to balance at once the lives of father and son and, more generally, the lessons of the intellect with those—in the end more telling—of experience. In conception, it is an ambitious attempt at a complex symbolical structure designed to orchestrate at every level the theme of the historical continuity or discontinuity, meaning or meaninglessness, of "the only animal to know that it must die." Malraux is trying to weld disparate elements: narrative, intellectual, and lyrical, into a poem on man.

A short introductory section presents us with the narrator in a makeshift prisoner-of-war camp in Chartres. The juxtaposition of the Europe of the cathedrals with the sound of German tanks, and the age-old acceptance of the prisoners in the face of this disaster, lead him to brood on the mystery of man with which, as a writer, he has been "obsessed for the past ten years." As a support for this meditation, he sets out to recount significant episodes in the life of his father, whose experience from the German side in the previous conflict seems in some ways to have anticipated his own. Already, therefore, we have the search for continuity within discontinuity. To balance this opening section there is a final one, also printed in italics. Reverting to his present situation, the narrator describes a tank attack in which he had been engaged prior to the collapse and ends with a lyrical sense of the common humanity and solidarity of men, as of the "miracle" of life itself.

Within this framework, the body of the work presents three separate but related moments in the life of the narrator's father, Vincent Berger. This young German orientalist starts his teaching at the University of Constantinople in 1908 with a course on Nietzsche and the "philosophy of action." As the term itself may suggest, the "action" interests him more than the "philosophy" and he is soon drawn into a romantic kind of secret diplomatic activity on behalf of his country. On the one hand he is presented as something of a "shaman," one who does not easily accept the given reality of things but who is prepared to go to great lengths—like the prophetic, priestly, traditional Eastern shaman himself—to impose a dream or a truth upon the world. On the other hand, he is presented as intelligent, lucid, honest, and lacking any self-indulgence: not just an idle night-time dreamer but one of those serious or "dangerous" men, as T. E. Lawrence calls them, who "dream by day."

In the first of these three episodes, then, we find this oddly familiar figure operating on the complicated diplomatic chess board of the pre-1914 Balkans, acquiring a legend as a grey eminence to the romantic, Napoleonic young military leader Enver Pasha (who in the novel also incorporates part of the actual historical role of Mustafa Kemal Bey) and his Young Turk movement. Like the early adventurer, Vincent has no seriously developed patriotic or other motivation toward this activity and, like some sort of "lucid" sleepwalker, is too concerned with the mechanics of the problem to see it in perspective. So it is that he commits himself to Enver's Pan-Turanian pipedream of bringing together all the Turkoman peoples into a vast Young Turk empire with its capital at Samarkand, trails across Central Asia in a vain attempt to revive the old blood alliance, and is only delivered from his obsession when he is attacked by a madman.

Inevitably enough, this episode has been seen in over-simplified terms as an allegory of Malraux's "break with Communism." However, we are told that for Vincent "the social problem had not arisen" and this young alter ego is obviously closer to the adventurers of the early novels than to the revolutionary heroes of the 1930s; he reads like a composite of the mythical early Malraux, his heroes Perken and Garine, and Lawrence of Arabia. The pattern and quality of this venture really come closest to the basic, "shamanistic" fable of defeat laid down initially in *Royaume farfelu*. If Malraux takes the quest for self so far back, it is because he is less concerned with the external value of a specific "action" than with trying, more fundamentally, to establish himself in projection as a particular human type. It is also of course because, in so doing, he is at once driven back to the original "trauma" from which, in transposition, the young Vincent's dreamlike commitment-within-estrangement proceeds.

The next "encounter with man" takes Vincent on the eve of the 1914 war to an international colloquy at the Altenburg priory in his native Alsace, presided over by his faintly fraudulent professorial uncle Walter Berger. Malraux indeed, though the ideas are taken very seriously, is ironical about this closed world of intellectuals in which "an idea never proceeded from a fact, always from another idea"; he was amusing himself here with a gentle takeoff of the Pontigny colloquies in which, like so many authors from the Gallimard "stable," he took part between the wars. The occasion is darkened at once by the recent, mysterious suicide of Vincent's father and, above all, by the impact upon the nineteenth-century evolutionist thinking of these men— some of whom had leaned towards a Hegelian kind of Pan-Germanism as ludicrous as Enver's Pan-Turanianism—of a new trend toward pluralist thinking in history and ethnology. Finally, in the third episode, we find Berger as an intelligence officer with the German army on the Vistula front in 1915. He is revolted by the moral blackmail used during the interrogation of a suspected woman spy, and finally sickened by a gas attack against the Russians which so disturbs and humiliates the German infantrymen themselves that they defiantly carry their afflicted enemies back toward their own lines. Vincent himself joins in this spontaneous protest and is gassed as a result— although we are given to understand that he will recover.

Such are the bare bones of *Les Noyers de l'Altenburg,* yet another of his novels which Malraux describes briskly in private as *"mal foutu."* In fact, as the Turkish section shows, he remains an excellent straight narrator, while the Altenburg colloquy is deftly handled. Again, as in many of the scenes describing nature, he often attains to a new kind of sober dignity and harmony of style, as also to a new lyricism. Even so, the attempt to order disparate elements into a symbolical and poetic whole does not go without overlap and some confusion, while there often seems to be a gap between the concrete situation and the lyricism. To some extent, the weakness may be due to the technical difficulties of such an ambitious enterprise. Even if it is conceived as a kind of poem, a work of fiction creates certain expectations, and it is clear that Malraux's structure does not allow him to deal adequately with the moral issues raised by his very special situation. Again, the amount of detail given in the Vincent Berger episodes makes the convention that the narrator is reconstituting these from notes left by his father seem a little thin. Also, this secondhand narration may be partly responsible for the loss in dramatic immediacy. And reasons other than the technical may be found. For example, the rather crude caricature of the German professor who has perfected the poison gas may be the effect of haste, or of the exhaustion of 1941, or of a new impatience with fiction projection.

For all this, it remains that the real weakness of the work lies at the central point of application of this search for self: in the portrait of Vincent Berger. The scenes of action in which he figures, "pure Malraux" in conception though they are, seem relatively lifeless. Locked in a dream in Central Asia, quiet before the suspected spy, slow-reacting as when he is wandering around after the gas attack, Vincent seems oddly silent, remote, and unreal. It is possible, of course, that Malraux is so close to the character that he simply takes him too much for granted. Or one might say that he had previously been projecting himself through his characters toward *future* attitudes, whereas he is here projecting backward into the past. And yet Vincent is obviously central to the whole ambitious conception, while Malraux, by placing him in a time and in places not known to himself—and this involved research—has set up the character with due regard for artistic distancing. Given Malraux's remarkable gifts as a novelist and given the special context of the search for self in this work, it is possible that his failure to bring Vincent alive is of particular and sad significance. It may be that he got back to the "trauma" but could neither assume it nor break it; that the "dominated writer" is already settling for Spengler and for a secondary, intellectual treatment of his privileged themes, compensating for lack of centrality with lyrical rhetoric; that on this final rock of self a major imaginative writer has foundered.

At all events, the interest of *Les Noyers* lies less in its central character than in the overall "trial of man" of which the Altenburg colloquy itself, at which the ethnologist Möllberg plays prosecutor, is both the pivot and the image.

Some of Möllberg's examples were taken by Malraux from the writings of Leo Frobenius, but unlike Spengler Frobenius was a "diffusionist" and Möllberg's perspective, in essence, is Spenglerian. He instances societies ignorant of such elementary Western assumptions as our idea of time, or even our explanation of birth, but which nevertheless had their own coherence. For each social structure is built upon a particular central idea or myth, he argues, and these may vary so much from culture to culture as to make men belonging to each different *in kind*. Nor is there any point in saying that there is still a basic similarity between a peasant in ancient Egypt and his counterpart in modern Alsace, for the tragic irony is that the more a man participates in his own culture—the more fully "human" he becomes through its specific knowledge, skills, and arts— the more he distances himself from those of other cultures. So there is no "fundamental man" of any significance and no fixed "human nature," while the "history" so dear to some of his listeners is little more than a mirage.

The "case against man" is not a purely intellectual one, since the emptiness of Vincent's Eastern venture combines with the presentation of war as a fatality to suggest also the vanity of human action. However, it is largely through a set of intuitions and poetic affirmations that Malraux seeks to redress the balance.

To begin with, there is the insight of Vincent Berger which provides the title. Pointing to walnut statues of different periods in the Altenburg library, Möllberg hammers home his point by saying that, even though they may be made of the same wood, there is no "fundamental walnut" underlying their different forms: only dead logs. Yet as he walks alone at sunset towards the ancient, *living* trees of the Altenburg, Vincent senses in their tenacious, *intermediate* reality "a will and a metamorphosis without end" which make Möllberg's symbolical alternative seem merely academic. And this central insight is supported throughout by elements designed to suggest that whether "vertically," in time, or "horizontally," across barriers of nationality or class or language, man is one. Does not the sense of the unity of physique and of destiny of the Bergers of Reichbach, or the way in which the prisoners of war revert to the statuesque simplicity of medieval men, or the unchanging landscape itself, argue for human continuity? Does not the instinctive revolt of the German infantrymen against the use of gas suggest an awareness of man's dignity, and therefore of his fundamental nature? Does not the transcendent purity of the song of the mad Nietzsche in the darkened railway carriage, as recounted by Walter Berger, or the confident irony of the old woman smiling at the end on disaster, suggest that "the only animal to know that it must die" can be stronger than madness, and even than death?

The stages of the psychological movement involved are: total estrangement from life, leading to an almost extraterrestrial sense of an empty freedom, producing a sense of the gratuitousness of life—transmuted suddenly into a sense of the uniqueness of life, soon apprehended as the "miracle" of life. This then leads to the lyrical intuition of a great "gift" and of "a secret which would have been no less poignant even if man had been immortal." There are indeed lyrical moments toward the end of *Les Noyers* when this death-obsessed writer comes close to burying death.

Yet the very range of this faintly jerky psychological "metamorphosis" is indicative. Malraux may set up a cyclical situation in order to prove, against Spengler, that the cycle is open and not closed, but the very setting up leaves him from the outset fighting on his opponent's terms. He cannot really "argue"; he must, psychologically and poetically, transcend. And the lyricism itself—or, more precisely, the imperfect fusion of the lyricism with the concrete totality of the work—combines with the lack of centrality of Vincent Berger to suggest that, as he approaches the next round of his "struggle with the angel," the new and moving balance achieved in Malraux's final novel is a fragile one.

CHAPTER 8

In Search of Fundamental Man (II): Art as Transcendence

MALRAUX'S writings on art, both wide-ranging and controversial as they are, clearly raise many technical questions in the interpretation of collective or individual styles which cannot be developed here. My main concern is to bring out the nature and purpose of these writings, to situate them in relation to Malraux's overall enterprise as a writer, and to consider the validity of the larger argument underlying them in the context—already established in the previous chapter—of the explicit search for "fundamental man" which marks this phase of his career.

I The Nature of the Art Writings

At the simple bibliographical level, the writings on art may present a confusing picture. Quite apart from the overlap within the texts themselves, and the further complication of the publication of fragments in reviews, there is the fact that the three separately published volumes of *La Psychologie de l'art* were revised and reissued in one volume in 1951 under the new title of *Les Voix du silence*. Again, Malraux, who has remained closely associated with the publisher Gallimard, has acted as adviser for series of art publications and has therefore written prefaces as general editor as well as introducing, for example, his own three-volume album *Le Musée imaginaire de la sculpture mondiale*. In this situation, it may be helpful to indicate the three more important texts.

Since *Les Voix du silence* itself is difficult, if not so impenetrable as some have made out, the best introduction to Malraux's approach is probably his essay on Goya, *Saturne*. Here he studies Goya's realism from the Caprichos etchings up to the final Black

116

Paintings in order to argue the metaphysical obsession of this rationalist with what Malraux, perhaps a little confusingly, calls the "sacred" and the "demon." By the "sacred," he means the supernatural or the suprarational, or simply those forces greater than man which constitute "destiny"; by the "demon," or "devil", he means essentially human evil: "that force in man which seeks to destroy him." The interest of *Saturne* is that the larger argument of *Les Voix du silence* is here conveniently concentrated within the close study of a single artist. Goya, indeed, is an important test case for Malraux's theory to the extent that he displays the necessary break of genius with an existing artistic tradition, shows that the meaning even of self-conscious "realism" goes far beyond representation or illusion and, above all, exemplifies the artist's "conquest" over "destiny" by providing a kind of agnostic equivalent of the great religious arts of the past.

This driving theme of the artist's conquest over destiny through rupture with an existing tradition and transcendence of the real receives its grand orchestration in *Les Voix du silence,* which remains the central statement of Malraux's aesthetic or metaphysic of art. A supplementary text of considerable interest is *La Métamorphose des dieux,* of which the first volume—the second has yet to appear—was published in 1957. Here, in a rather more tightly organized and chronological fashion, Malraux amplifies his view that great art always looks beyond appearance through a study of the transmutation of the "sacred" in Greek art and in European Christian art up to the turning point of the Renaissance. However, it is perhaps in the next volume that the real challenge to the consistency of his overall approach will present itself, if only because he will then have to deal more fully with the considerable problem posed by modern nonfigurative art. At all events, we are inevitably concerned essentially here with the broad pattern laid down in *Les Voix du silence.*

The first thing to be said about Malraux's approach is simply that he displays an astonishing knowledge of world art, whether ancient or modern, Western or Eastern—so much so, indeed, that the great Bernard Berenson was led to demur in his last diaries at the suggestion that his own range was not so great.[1] Again, a kind of impassioned insight, often expressing itself in

a startling but suggestive juxtaposition, inspires some brilliant
formal analyses of the development of styles. Where he feels
a special sympathy with a painter, as with El Greco, Georges
de La Tour, or Rembrandt, he can be highly illuminating; in
the essay on Goya, where he has room to develop, he operates
by a kind of empathetic fusion with his subject which makes
his tragic yet somberly triumphant account not only impressive but moving. It should be said also that Malraux displays
considerable familiarity with techniques. Finally, to a high
generosity of mind, he obviously adds stylistic resources which
few writers in this field could hope to command.

Yet these writings have probably given rise to more controversy than any previous moment of Malraux's controversial
career. At one level, since they were published through the
Cold War period, the division of opinion has been broadly
political. There were many who saw here a lyrical antirational-
ism and pessimism which confirmed Malraux's "betrayal of
the Left" and of traditional humanism; it is against this background that Claude-Edmonde Magny's description of Malraux's "Imaginary Museum" in 1948 as "a Buchenwald of the
plastic arts" acquires its full flavor.[2] As against this, there were
many—including some right-wing Catholic reviewers rather
obviously hoping to "annex" this "ex-revolutionary"—who saw
rather a new and profound concern for the larger interests
of man.

At a more general level, there has been a broad division of
opinion of a different kind. A number of favorable literary
critics have treated Les Voix du silence and La Métamorphose
des dieux as key works of the century, while many general
readers—whether because of the wider interest in art due to
color reproduction, or because a certain cultural disquiet since
the war has led to a new interest in universal history—have
responded warmly to Malraux's attempt to integrate discussion
of art into the common culture. On the other hand, some professional art historians have been cool to the point of accusing
him of obscurity, faulty method, intellectual charlatanism, and
wholesale plagiarism. He has been largely dismissed by E. H.
Gombrich, among others, and paid the rather fierce compliment
of a monumental onslaught in three volumes by Georges
Duthuit, ruthlessly entitled Le Musée inimaginable.

It is not difficult to see why some art historians, even beyond their intellectual objections, should be irritated by a work like *Les Voix du silence*. I do not incidentally see any professional jealousy here, though there has doubtless been some suspicion of Malraux's Gaullist attitudes and, while he himself is not to be blamed for this, of the rather portentous flummery into which the "legend" flowered at this time—a large front-page photograph in one of the more excitable literary weeklies of "the passionate hand of André Malraux," for example, is hardly calculated to further serious discussion. But the real irritant is that the work is neither physically so presented nor internally so organized as to follow the usual procedures of intellectual argument. Malraux does not acknowledge the labors of his predecessors, even where he is building on them. He is not inclined to marshall historical evidence in the normal manner, and tends to jump toward the large generalization without having established the intermediates. If he often seems obscure to the point of being suspected of high-class shadow boxing, it is also because he is similarly allusive and elliptical in his style, even where he may be dealing with a handful of artists or schools within the single sentence. In fact, his general tendency is not so much to demonstrate as to proclaim, to be not simply lyrical but oracular.

Yet the antirationalist, antihistorical bent of Malraux's procedure, or even his nonacknowledgment of sources, is not at all to be seen as charlatanism. Nor indeed, at one level, is the question of the newness of his ideas in terms of art history of too much importance. It may be true that his starting point of the "Imaginary Museum" and of the "metamorphosis" brought about by photographic reproduction was established by Walter Benjamin, that this and other of his concepts were anticipated by Henri Focillon, or that the idea of the independence of "forms" was developed by Élie Faure. They may well, also be debts to Wilhelm Worringer, Émile Mâle and René Grousset, among others. But to pose the question of Malraux's originality in a simply scholarly fashion is at once to miss the impact of the larger influences leading him toward these sources and to take *Les Voix du silence* for what it is not.

For what we have here, strangely, is perhaps as much a work *of* art as a work on art. It is hardly conceived as "art history," though Malraux seems very familiar with this. Nor is it really a "psychology of art," for all the original title, in either the technical or the speculative sense—Malraux's long-standing aversion to the latter kind of psychology is sharper than ever. What is involved is rather, as in *La Condition humaine,* a "metapsychology" in that he is trying to establish the artist's "conquest" over "destiny," while fighting against any Freudian reduction of his achievement. Yet this does not make it strictly a "philosophy of art," if only because Malraux is in the end not interested here in art or in the artist *as such.* He is concerned rather with art as the voice of a culture or an age, and with the artist as the exemplar of Man.

While this obviously brings his inquiry into Spengler's own area of the "philosophy of history," his procedures remain such that one would be driven to speak of an allusive or poetic ontology of history. Yet this still does not convey the passion or the pathos of the work. To listen to Malraux's own deliberate, heavily rhetorical recording of the concluding pages of *Les Voix du silence* is to remember that he is fond of talking about the "preaching" of Nietzsche and to think, somewhat eerily, of the great sermons of Bossuet. Eerily, because Bossuet had after all in the seventeenth century the historical reality of the Church behind him whereas Malraux, in a very different age, sees the problem underlying the whole of his work as being "how to make man aware that he can build his greatness, without religion, upon the nothingness that crushes him."[3] So it is that there is a lonely, tormented quality to the oracular lyricism. Malraux indeed, in the face of this fantastic pageant of the arts of the planet which he conjures up, seems at times like a latter-day Saint Anthony wrestling with visions in the desert. What he emerges with, once again, is a poem on "fundamental Man."

To say this, of course, is not to suggest that Malraux's work on art is immune to intellectual criticism. On the contrary, it is to ask even more sharply why it *had* to be written in this form.

As we shall see, the reason is that, at the intellectual and perhaps also the emotional level, Malraux was walking a tight-rope across a void.

II *The Dialectical Metamorphosis*

The context of Malraux's aesthetic is what he calls the Imaginary Museum: the fact that through photographic reproduction we now have access for the first time in history to the artistic heritage of the planet. From the potentially endless confrontation of works of all ages in this veritable empyrean of art—in which a Picasso, say, can rub shoulders with the Etruscans—emerge not only new oppositions and affinities, but a whole new perspective. The hegemony of the Greco-Roman tradition is swept away, the classical European painting which had been the traditional yardstick seen to be an exception. As against the older unilinear view, with its high peaks and dark ages, Malraux argues that what were once seen as retrogressive or barbaric arts—such as the post-classical Byzantine or Gallo-Roman—are in fact new and high stylizations in their own right. Styles, in a word, are to be approached on the assumption that they are equal in dignity.

This enables Malraux to move from any classification based on representational skills toward a broad metaphysical distinction between humanist arts, which hold man to be a value, and sacred arts, which are defined primarily in terms of the rejection of the world of appearance. Insofar as they have sought essentially to give form to the forces dominating man, religious arts have always been antirealist and "antihuman." Two apparent exceptions here, Greek art and medieval Christian art, are treated as special cases. Greek art reconciled man with the eternal by humanizing the gods; medieval art did likewise, to the extent that Christianity stressed redemption and a divine possibility in man. The sacred arts, of course, have predominated in history. It is in this perspective that Malraux suggests that modern art, insofar as it also rejects resemblance and idealization, is itself a new kind of "sacred art."

Within this framework he sets out to free the artist—and, by extension, "Man"—from historical, social, and psychological determinisms. His key word is *arracher*, his aesthetic one of transcendence through rupture or separation. Separation of artist and individual, style and vision, art and culture, and art and history.

The artist, to begin with, transcends himself as an individual.

As a man, he may be swayed by instinct or feeling or the un-conscious, but in his art he dominates, possesses, gives form to these things: he is free. His achievement is not reducible to any physiological or psychological explanation—Beethoven's deaf-ness at the time of the Ninth Symphony, or the "vulture ob-session" which Freud lent to Leonardo da Vinci—for no bio-graphical explanation can account for what really matters: the *quality* of the work. Again, the artist is not to be defined roman-tically as being "inspired," or being more "sensitive," or having deeper feelings than other people; he may be less sensitive than a young girl, while the expression of deep feeling may produce atrocious art. If an artist wants to express deep grief, for example, he can cry like the rest of us. If he is led by the experience to paint a picture, he is seeking rather to transmute it in such a way as to place it beyond itself in the separate, or "autonomous" world of art. In fact, "the artist creates less in order to express himself than he expresses himself in order to create." And, in creating, he can so rise above himself that, as Malraux puts it, "Buonarotti is not Michelangelo": individual and artist are not one.

Nevertheless, at least as artist, he is always *conscious* in his work. Even the Romantics, Malraux insists, were always aware of the specific nature of their art. What then does this tran-scendent artistic consciousness strive to achieve? Not some sort of ideal Beauty, a subjective myth which varies from age to age. Nor even, for all that certain Impressionists or others may have said, a more accurate way of *seeing* the world. The artist does not necessarily see reality more sharply or differently from others—Cézanne hardly saw in terms of volume, any more than Modigliani thought that people had long necks. "Every artist of genius," Malraux insists, "finds his expression of the world not through his vision but through his style." From which it follows, of course, that the artist does not imitate nature. Art is not the rendering or the reproduction of reality, but the transfiguration of reality. Even the straightforward or self-conscious realist—a Courbet, a Corot, a Vermeer—is never simply transcribing, but *stylizing*. "Insofar as it is art," says Malraux firmly, "*all* realism is a *rectification* of reality." Art is invention, and the important thing is style.

Malraux is therefore seeking to establish the transcendent

freedom of the artist by asserting the *specificity* of art. The artist is seen as being bound neither by instinct, nor by his own psychological reality, nor by external nature, nor by an ideal style, nor by the expression of feeling. How then, within the terms of this "metapsychology," does he actually proceed in the autonomous world of art? He enters into it, in the first place, because he is moved more by pictures or statues than by the world itself, and he begins in effect with *pastiche*. But if he is a true artist he will soon sense a conflict between the style he has chosen to imitate and the embryo of his own developing style: his "initial schema." He will then break away, slowly devour the parent style, and gradually, by a constant process of meta-morphosing forms, achieve his own style. This is a formal rather than a personal or historical progression, but once he has achieved his own independent world of form within the specific world of art he will have transcended life, contingency, and time.

So it is that art, more generally, is an "antidestiny." History is impure; art is the quintessence of the meaning of the human adventure in time: the transcendent "song of history." It may be true that the great collective styles have reflected the values of their civilization, but they have not done so directly or neces-sarily contemporaneously. A painter lives in his own age, shares its beliefs, and may even conceive his art in terms of those beliefs; yet "*as creator*, the artist does not belong to the collec-tivity that is subject to a culture, but to the new one that is taking shape." His art relates him rather, beyond time, to the "eternal creative power of man." And "all true art," in that it serves "an obscurely or vehemently elected part of man," is a striving toward transcendence.

It is true, of course, that in history this tended to go hand in hand with a formally religious transcendence, whereas, as Mal-raux constantly reminds us, ours is the first civilization in his-tory to be without a transcendence. Instead of a monolithic faith we have the Imaginary Museum, and the sharp sense of history which goes with our agnosticism has reduced the abso-lutes that informed these sacred arts of the past to "the small change of the absolute." What then of modern and abstract art? Insofar as the artist still strains beyond appearance toward his own independent world—and insofar as Malraux sees ours as an anxious civilization no longer sure of man's meaning—

this new and agnostic "sacred art" does in a special sense have its own elected "supreme value": "the ancient will to create an autonomous world, *reduced for the first time to itself alone.*" Art, in a word, has become its own transcendence.

Having separated art from culture and from history, therefore, Malraux tries to bridge the gap through the idea of *quintessential* expression, or transcendence. And the continuity which he obviously needs to counter Spengler's view of cultures as separate, closed cycles is provided through the idea of a complex relational metamorphosis. There is the individual artist metamorphosing nature and metamorphosing the forms he had chosen to pastiche in the pursuit of his own style—which may then become the starting point for another, possibly endless, series of metamorphoses. At the collective level, there are even the so-called retrogressive styles, *not* degrading established forms but metamorphosing them as part of the sequence of this indirect, transmigratory, self-transcending transmission of values. Finally, there is the grandiose dialectical metamorphosis of these essences within the Imaginary Museum itself. For the confrontation of masterpieces of all times and places is a continually fructifying "dialogue" through which perspectives are inflected, enlarged, and transformed. The Museum is *alive*, with these "voices of silence."

It is here that the eternality of the artist's gesture is manifest, and here that we possess what is noblest in the civilizations of the past. Look at these statues in the Museum. Their makers, known or unknown, may all be dispersed in dust, but these statues are "more Egyptian than were the Egyptians, more Christian than the Christians, more Michelangelo than Michelangelo himself—more human than the world." Above death and oblivion, beyond the prison of history, there is at least this one domain of quality and transcendence warmed by the "fraternity of masterpieces." Art remains alive as the expression of the nobility and the permanence of man—and, thereby, as a basis for "the first universal humanism."

III *Victory in the Void*

It should be clear, even from so condensed a summary, that Malraux raises a host of problems of great interest. I believe also that much of what he says about the creative process is challenging and valuable, even if he tends to overschematize it in generalization. However, I consider that the merits of the work lie in the end in particular insights rather than in the implicit overall argument with which—since Malraux makes so much hinge upon it—we must essentially be concerned.

If he does not cite sources, there is inevitably one title mentioned in *Les Voix du silence*: *The Decline of the West*. In the last chapter, I suggested that "Spengler" was really a form of shorthand for a fundamental private dilemma. It will therefore not be surprising if, in the present context, he emerges as being for Malraux the problematic center of the whole intellectual tradition which marked him so decisively in his early years.

It was in Germany rather than in France that systematic art philosophy flourished during the nineteenth century, and its Expressionist critics who were setting the pace in this field when Malraux came to it at the end of World War I. Their view of art as the essential expression of a culture parallels Spengler's idea of the "culture-soul," but of course both he and they are continuous with a lengthy German tradition. Behind them there is Hegel, a distant source of the idea of the autonomy of art, with his "spirit of the age" and his heavily systematic historical dialectic. There is also Nietzsche, another strong influence on Spengler himself, with his prophetic stance, his view of art as a transcendent justification of life, and his aspiration to a "transvaluation of all values" following upon the "death of God." Beyond this again—and Nietzsche's "Superman" himself can be traced back through precise stages in literature and in philosophy—there is the Romantic idea of the uniqueness of the genius: the tormented, but inspired visionary acting as torch in the new and dark European unknown following upon the collapse of universal religion along with the old social order. This whole (and far from unilinear) tradition was obviously mediated through the uneasy aftermath of war in a host of secondary ways, but it is in relation to this that Malraux's Promethean aesthetic of the genius as "Man," with its themes of transcendence and dialectical metamorphosis, may most clearly be seen. And since the estranged young Malraux was interested beyond art in Man, the whole intellectual current crystallized for him in the originally justifying, but finally challenging figure of Spengler.

Indeed there are moments in these writings when Malraux seems like some sort of Romantic, Nietzschean, and even Dionysian spirit lost in the final Spenglerian "winter" or "Megalopolitan" stage of European civilization, calling lyrically to his fellows through the "night" to see beyond their world-weary skepticism, empty socialized individualism, and bankrupt scientism, in order to forge some new and unifying, if tragic, vision of Man. And the poignancy springs from the grim irony that in this spiritual struggle he so often seems to be wearing his adversary's clothes. The very rhapsodic sweep, with its great antitheses, recalls Spengler's idea of the historian as "genius" or "artist," while so many other Spenglerian lines of thought—his view of a cultural style as a Destiny, his description of the inner motivation of the "culture-soul" as a "Destiny-idea," or his relegation of science to the status of local and transitory "myth"—seem to stand behind the writing almost like the bars of a cage.

For Malraux's intellectual dilemma is extraordinary to the point of being desperate. If another writer wished to refute Spengler he might, quite apart from attacking Spengler's intellectual procedures, try to argue continuity through the transmission of scientific knowledge and philosophical ideas—Plato rather than whitened Greek statues—and perhaps end up by pointing to the rather obviously increasing "Westernization" of the whole planet. Or if he wished to demonstrate the accessibility of the past in relation to the arts alone—in effect, making his task rather more difficult—he might concentrate on literature or on a collective, functional art such as architecture, rather than deal solely with the plastic arts. In practice, however, he would be tending to demonstrate the artificiality of Malraux's very question as to whether or not "Man is dead," and to operate in terms of the modern agnostic rationalist humanism which Malraux—antirationalist like Spengler himself—denies. It is of course *because* of this denial that Malraux *needs* to refute Spengler. And because of it also, by a second irony, that he cannot fashion the weapons with which to do so convincingly—so that he is left saying after the publication of *Les Voix du silence* that "the only serious one among them is Spengler."

The original "trauma" for which Spengler is as it were the code name is still present in that Malraux, in effect, is trying to get beyond *La Tentation de l'Occident* without retracting its basic postulates. At the time of the art writings he was saying that Europe needed a transcendence, and that the task of the next century would be to reinvent its gods. Meanwhile, he was groping toward an alternative humanism, or agnostic religion, which would be appropriate to what he saw as a new age of fatality or destiny. As the foundation stone for this he needed some kind of finality or transcendent element in man, and saw the hope of this in artistic genius. Whence the battle on one flank, not only against Freudian reduction of the artist's conquest, but against any social or historical determinism, Marxian or otherwise: he must protect the purity and the transcendence over history of the artist, even at the cost of separating him from his historical self. It should be remembered, not only that the artist symbolizes Man, but that Malraux was writing during the Cold War period. Where he did not equate modern agnostic humanism with an empty skepticism expressing itself in a futile individualism, he was inclined to equate it with what he saw as its remaining "strong" form: Marxist determinism. It is for these related reasons that he may seem to present history as the mere occasion for art.

The trouble, of course, is that over this self-constructed void he now has to perform a most extraordinary balancing act— one rendered the more difficult in that, by so firmly throwing out historical determinism, he might seem to have thrown out the continuity which went with it: the baby with the bath water. For his whole operation is clearly pointless unless he can nevertheless establish the artist's transcendence as being *representative,* and as having a general validity going back through time. It is for this reason that he has to fight his second battle on the opposite flank against Spengler. If he looks more than vulnerable on his "tightrope," therefore, it is because he must somehow establish the representativeness and continuity in time—in effect, however indirectly, the *historicity*—of what is given as a highly specific *suprahistorical* transcendence "wrested" by the artist from a tradition, from the values of his time, and even from his own reality as a man.

The ambiguity proceeding from this self-division infects criticism itself to the point that he can be accused at once of "historicism" and of being antihistorical. His will to make art stand for culture as a whole while yet insisting on the conquering, individualistic character of genius inevitably raises questions throughout. Does he adequately define genius, or the master-piece, or the artist's "initial schema"? Does he not oversimplify by his distinction between humanist and sacred arts, and by equating spirituality with the rejection of appearances? Does he not tend to personalize the great styles, and sometimes to define them in terms of a single characteristic? Is modern ab-stract art not radically different as regards its place and function within the culture from the sacred arts of the past? Is it not to some extent dictated negatively by the very invention of pho-tography which underlies the Imaginary Museum, and is it not to some extent also a function of that individualism, sanctioned by an agnostic culture, which Malraux deplores? However, I wish only to point to two problems which, given Malraux's overall perspective, might seem to be central.

The first concerns the pivotal idea of the Imaginary Museum itself, this new photographic temple of art. Now the Museum, in that works are admitted on the sole criterion of style and independently of their historical context, function, or physical dimensions, may look like the very image of the timelessness, freedom, and metamorphosis of art. But of course the Museum is not simply a warehouse for world art; it is necessarily selec-tive. The criterion of style, equally necessarily, is interpreted by us. And the selection, since the Museum is itself a function of our untranscended age, is made in terms of what Malraux sees as our "culture of interrogation." Yet he himself insists that the situation of the first civilization in history to be without a transcendence is a new one; in other words, it is itself a his-torical phenomenon and one which may be superseded. So although Malraux is not prepared to evaluate past arts directly in terms of their own cultures, he is evaluating them, like mod-ern abstract art, in terms of his own reading of ours. His whole attempt to present art as transcendence over history might seem to be revolving within a rather narrow historical instrumentalism.

The same circle of irony would seem to present itself when we examine the human content of the alternative continuity-within-metamorphosis with which Malraux seeks to support his new tragic humanism. How real, in fact, is the artist's victory over history, or destiny? In the first place, he is already separated humanly from his art, which is not tied to any feelings, perceptions, or ideas he may have wished to embody. His artistic "consciousness" is opposed to ordinary consciousness, and it is only as artist that he can achieve transcendence, not as individual. In the second place, he may have been working within some *common* transcendence or religious absolute; if so, the long sequence of metamorphosis will relativize and betray it. In the third place, even his transcendent artistic consciousness is dissolved like a drop in the ocean since the autonomous, transcendent forms he achieved in terms of it must have their meaning perpetually reinterpreted and altered by the process of confrontation and change, the continually self-creating relativism of the grand dialectical metamorphosis which culminates in our own Imaginary Museum. From the point of view of the living artist—who, after all, seems to hold out the only, and oblique, hope of transcendence for "Man"—is this freedom or dependence, an "antidestiny" or a fatality, a conquest over history or betrayal by history?

In *Les Noyers de l'Altenburg*, Malraux's quest for self led him to the original point of self-division; he seemed to achieve less a resolution than a lyrical transcendence or poetic balance. Here, in this more secondary, speculative onslaught on the problem called "Spengler," he appears, for all the incidental richness of the writing, to end up in Romantic subjectivism and hollowness. There is indeed, in the context of the striving informing his whole career, something sadly abstract and lonely about a "fraternity of masterpieces" which looks like a fraternity of infinitely changing, drifting ghosts.

CHAPTER 9

Malraux and Gaullism

"ON my right I have, and shall always have, André Malraux," wrote de Gaulle in his description of Fifth Republic cabinet meetings in the volume of memoirs published just before his death. "The presence at my side of this friend of genius and devotee of high destinies gives me the sense of being protected against the commonplace. The view which this incomparable witness holds of myself helps to strengthen my resolve."[1]

Over nearly a quarter of a century, from 1945 to 1969, Malraux's political activity was tied not only to the career of Charles de Gaulle, but to a deep sense of personal loyalty to this man who, as he has often said, maintained the honor of his defeated country through World War II "like an invincible dream." He became one of the general's few close personal friends and, whether in opposition or in government, enjoyed a rather privileged position among his followers. To some extent there were direct similarities between the two men. Both were solitary, proud, and at the private level highly disinterested; both were visionaries obsessed by history, impatient of present complexity or compromise and, thereby, somewhat contemptuous of professional politics; both were ambitious and prepared to envisage exceptional means of action. To some extent also this was an attraction of opposites, or mirror images: of the independent "revolutionary" and the independent traditionalist, of the myth-making novelist of action tempted by the real, and the achieved man of action tempted by the myth and the pen.

From the Liberation to their departure together in 1969—through the Cold War, their return to power after the army-supported Algiers revolt of May 1958, and the backlash of the "Revolution" of May 1968—their association was a spectacular and a checkered one.

130

I *From World War to Cold War*

A vast, empty stage, a small dark figure dwarfed by the tricolor with its tall Cross of Lorraine, a curiously lonely and lyrical eloquence inflating itself eerily at moments through the loud-speakers, while a largely lower-middle-class audience waited for the more obvious Cold War arguments, and bulky members of the *service d'ordre* chatted fitfully in the gangways: to see Malraux in action at one of his own stage-managed Vélodrome d'Hiver spectaculars in 1951—when de Gaulle's Rally of the French People was already on the decline—was a rather embarrassing experience.

The Rassemblement du Peuple Français, founded in April 1947, was a confused and turbulent antiparliamentary, semifascist movement, which was not only dangerously unclear as to its intentions, but intellectually undistinguished and politically inept. As the Cold War receded, it was gradually absorbed by the party system it had denounced until, in 1956, its remaining vote reverted largely to the right-wing demagogue and champion of the small shopkeepers Pierre Poujade—the symbol of the whole overgrown distributive sector which Malraux, ironically, had seen as inhibiting postwar economic recovery. It is not for nothing that de Gaulle should later have seen his R.P.F. as a blunder, or that Malraux should pass over this period in *Antimémoires*. But how, in the immediate, did his lonely oratory about Man and transcendence relate to this political phenomenon? How could he have told James Burnham in the interview of 1948 that it was "only among the Gaullists that there can develop the human attitude of which the liberal hero would be the symbol"—even if it was in Lawrence of Arabia that he saw the exemplar of this "new human type?"

In *Antimémoires* Malraux relates the circumstances of his first and strange meeting with de Gaulle in 1945. This was effected through a curious stratagem on the part of a well-meaning intermediary—left rather mysteriously nameless by Malraux, but presumably Gaston Palewski—who told de Gaulle that Malraux wanted to serve, and Malraux that de Gaulle was asking him to serve. It was as a result of this meeting that Malraux was in mid-August appointed a technical adviser, in which capacity he instituted opinion polls and explored his idea of introducing audiovisual techniques into French education. In the government arising out of the October election he became minister for information, though he continued to see himself as a "technician" rather than as a political figure proper. He was indeed a somewhat maverick and less than conventionally efficient minister, interesting himself chiefly in the reproduction of paintings for schools and in thinking out his project for Maisons de la Culture. However, he was only in office for some two months, since de Gaulle withdrew from the party battle—partly, no doubt, to hold himself "in reserve"—in January 1946.

If by this time the basis of Malraux's future support for the R.P.F. had already been laid, it should be said that the meeting with de Gaulle had come less as a revelation than as the crystallization of attitudes already apparent, for example, in the interview he gave Stéphane at the front in February 1945—during which he also declared his desire to "do something concrete." Malraux's journey toward Gaullism begins with the Resistance.

After his escape in 1940, he had in fact written to de Gaulle offering his services as an airman, but the letter—unknown to Malraux, who therefore assumed that his political past made him unacceptable in London—was lost in the clandestine network. Later on, as has been seen, he refused to join "that crowd of royalists" and suggested—after "a moment's reflection"—that his place might rather be with the Red Army. At this stage, of course, he had to define his stance in relation to what was by then a full-scale Euro-Asian conflict which made London seem somewhat marginal. Indeed, it is partly because the internal Resistance seemed relatively unimportant that he declined several early invitations to become active. But there was another reason for this reluctance, important in that it leads to the heart of the experience which brought Malraux, as he was to tell de Gaulle with little or no exaggeration, to "marry France."

Not inclined by temperament to serve in a subordinate position, Malraux showed great determination in running his own show in the Resistance, as his insistence on maintaining the formal independence of his Alsace-Lorraine Brigade was to demonstrate. And with this brigade he formed, as it were, that pact of leadership which went with his own faintly aristocratic, heroic myth of quality-in-fraternity. Whereas in 1940 he had seen rather the defeated, semi-indifferent conscript soldier, these men from the long-disputed provinces were volunteers fighting fiercely not only to regain their homes but to prove their Frenchness. In their hard, triumphant course toward Germany, Malraux earned his command by matching them in courage and in loyalty. It was very much on his own terms, as a leader—for the first time victoriously, and for the first time on home ground—that he achieved himself and avenged his private losses in the Resistance. And an exalted sense of France was to be the pivot of his political thinking thereafter. Malraux, with the emotional conviction of the prodigal returned from afar, had in some sense joined his own tribe.

This new nationalism—never a vulgar one since he was to argue that France had always been greatest when she had been most generous, outward-looking, and universalist in her values —was balanced, and negatively justified, by his hardening view of Soviet Russia. It should be stressed, if only to explain a certain edge of bitterness, that even during the Cold War this non-Marxist would insist in conversation that he was opposed to the Stalinist perversion of the revolution in Russia rather than to communism itself. Accordingly, his motto toward the end of the war had been: "everything *for* Russia, but nothing *from* Russia." However, he had been impressed at that time by the sheer size of the Red Army, and resentful at what he saw as an attempt by the French party to annex the Resistance movement politically through clever infiltration. "I don't mind allying myself, but I don't want to be burgled," he told Stéphane, and went on to suggest "pessimistically" that, given the strength of the Communists, the only viable possibility might be something akin to the British Labour party.

Accordingly, at the congress of the Mouvement de Libération Nationale in January 1945, he argued against a fusion with the largely Communist-dominated Front National which would, in effect, have transformed the Resistance into a vast Popular Front type of political party, demanding large-scale nationalization of the means of production. Malraux, characteristically, was opposed to a "party" as such. What he wanted to see was a pragmatic alliance which would retain the diversity, the fraternal spirit

and the energy of the Resistance—and be as free as possible
of political professionalism. If he spoke of putting an end to
capitalism and insisted on the nationalization of the banks, he
told Stéphane that he had simply chosen the banks as an obvious
example—and that the fundamental contradiction of society
was probably no longer the opposition between capitalism and
the proletariat. Interested much less in concrete policies than
in the metaphysical perspective and moral tone of what might
emerge, what he really dreamed of was a heroic kind of open,
antidogmatic, liberal-socialist approach which in terms of effectiveness would rival communism itself.

Heroic or not, this was still some way from his future Gaullism.
However, his brief period in government had persuaded him
that the national interest was being sacrificed to interparty
warfare within the coalition and, as the Cold War set in and
he came to feel that the danger of a new world conflict was
acute, he moved rapidly toward the tough solution. He believed
that Stalinist Russia represented a real physical threat to France,
that the Communist party was sabotaging postwar recovery,
that its very existence falsified the workings of the traditional
liberal democratic system, and that the leaders of the "Third
Force" coalition against both Communism and Gaullism were
simply time-serving "administrators of illusion" operating a system which they knew to be a "limitless lie." It was in this spirit
that Malraux became the R.P.F.'s "propaganda delegate": a
curiously independent stage manager largely dictating its presentation to the public, trying with difficulty to establish its
press, raising funds through spectacular subscription campaigns,
and, of course, acting as star performer at its immensely spectacular rallies.

So far, Malraux's progress toward Gaullism is not difficult to
follow. But why so much exaggeration at all levels? Why these
rallies set up at almost ruinous cost and in so grandiose a fashion
as practically to invite comparison with those of Nuremberg only
a few years before? Why the constant catastrophist invocation
of the atomic holocaust, the death of Europe and the death
of Man, wrapped up in talk about art which made the Cold
War seem at moments like some eerie, Wagnerian battle for
"the plastic inheritance of the world?" Why the insistence that

modern culture was dead, that reason had failed, that parliaments—as he told Burnham—"were a part of 19th century democracy?" Why, in fact, did Malraux behave like a combination of propaganda chief, prophet, and even sorcerer of the R.P.F.?

At one level, the reasons are of a tactical nature: that Malraux in rather different directions was gambling for high stakes. He felt that the situation was desperate, and that a massive impact must be made at once. At the same time, he knew that he was in a minority position within this confused right-wing grouping and, for all his talk about the meaninglessness of Right and Left, privately saw himself as making a heroic bid to impose a leftist revolutionary spirit upon it—which may explain the extent of his bitterness at the failure of intellectuals to support it. Ironically, this curious combination of reasons was to put him in a minority in the opposite direction in October 1947. Explicitly seeing the movement as an insurrectionist one, he wished it to seize power after its 38 percent vote in the municipal elections, but was overruled by de Gaulle—who declared against "illegality"—and by Jacques Soustelle himself. The stress of such a strange position was itself bound to lead to some verbal inflation.

In the end, however, the reasons are largely temperamental and personal. As director of propaganda, Malraux was in some sense living his own fiction, playing at *being* Garine. As orator bathing the Cold War in the lurid light of doom, destiny and the death of man, he was publicly projecting the private battle with Spengler which occupied him in his art writings at night. The two modes of his political rhetoric—the one caustically down-to-earth, the other darkly visionary—correspond closely to these two levels of expression of his own myth. But the stark fundamentalism of the one and the oppositional polemics of the other enabled him, in effect, to keep the concrete complexity of politics to some extent at arm's length. While he rejected political programs in favor of "objectives," these tend to boil down to the setting up of Maisons de la Culture, which was marginal, and to the suppression of the Communist party—which might have caused civil war.

Malraux's private anguish about Man and his obsession with art were undoubtedly real, but then so was the political situation in front of him. His Gaullism at this period emerges as a curious combination of nobility and self-indulgent opportunism, of realism and naïveté. One might say that few of his fellow intellectuals emerge with credit from this grim Cold War period, that in constantly defending the freedom of the artist he was symbolically defending the essential of democratic freedom, and that at a time when many on the Left refused to see the defects of Stalinist Russia Malraux did not. On the other hand, a cosmic catastrophism in the service of a political blank cheque, to the promise of the exercise of morally neutral values such as "will," "effectiveness," and "decisiveness," does not add up to responsible—or, in the event, rewarding—political behavior. In fact, he was something of an *enfant terrible* in France's postwar period.

By the mid-1950s Malraux, though still describing himself as a Gaullist, had come round to expressing sympathy for Pierre Mendès-France and for a distinctively different, liberal "New Left." And the crisis of 1958 was of a different order. The Cold War had passed, Europe was prosperous, and France itself on the way to an economic boom. If it was only this unique Algerian problem which could have brought him back to office, de Gaulle —who negotiated his ambiguous return with quite extraordinary skill—had clearly learned much from his earlier fiasco. Also, he was this time to *need* the "system" against the professional army and the *ultra* elements which had helped him back to power.

II   *Malraux and the Fifth Republic*

If in a broadcast of June 1962 de Gaulle was to describe the Algiers *putsch* of May 13, 1958 as "an enterprise on the part of usurpers prepared to plunge the whole of France into civil war," this is not at all what he said at the time. All was ambiguity and confusion.

On June 1, 1958, Malraux became a minister attached directly to the general, and was then for some weeks in charge of information. It was in January 1959, when de Gaulle officially became president of the new Republic, with Michel Debré as prime minister, that he was appointed minister of state in charge of cultural affairs.

The complex and distinctive role which he was to play over the next decade is in fact not easily defined. Primarily, this is simply because Malraux was Malraux. By a curious paradox of which he himself was perfectly aware, the greater reality of this role lay in the extent to which it was seen as personal and symbolical. He never joined the new Gaullist party and, by 1968, was the only minister in office never to have sought an electoral mandate. Within this right-wing and initially disturbing regime, he represented not only the voice of culture but a certain moral guarantee for many of those in opposition. When he traveled abroad on behalf of his country, he automatically carried his own prestige as a writer—and his own legend—along with him.

A second difficulty about defining Malraux's role is that, for all this symbolical element, he did in fact engage in politics, both directly and indirectly. His activity thus tends also to reflect the difference between the first and second phases of this decade of Gaullist rule. The first, up to the Évian settlement of March 1962, was a dramatic and violent period dominated by the war in Algeria. The next six years, on the other hand, were to constitute a proudly nationalist phase marked by internal achievement, the French nuclear deterrent, and de Gaulle's will to an independent world role in the face of the two Great Powers. This, of course, was violently interrupted by the events of May 1968, which called in question many features of the régime—not excluding Malraux's conception of culture.

While the cultural and the political thus remain closely intertwined, I shall attempt first to deal with the more directly political aspect of Malraux's activity, considering briefly in turn his speeches at home, his representative visits abroad, and his role as "guarantee to the Left."

It was Malraux who organized the first great mass meeting of the referendum campaign in September 1958, symbolically—and unwisely, as the ensuing violence showed—choosing the Place de la République for the occasion. De Gaulle is said to have been displeased. However the choice, like Malraux's rather exalted introductory invocation of the Convention, Valmy, and Austerlitz, is already indicative of the intention governing his political speeches up to the end of the war in Algeria. He was

seeking, through historical references going back through Danton
or Saint-Just to Joan of Arc, not only to revitalize French
patriotism, but to establish the legitimacy of the new régime
within the tradition of the First Republic and of the Resistance.
If he set up an Association for the Fifth Republic before the
November elections of 1962, and continued to be prominent
at election "spectaculars" thereafter, it was with the new intention
of meeting the increasing challenge of the traditional parties
in opposition. However, he was now overshadowed in the
matter of persuasion by de Gaulle himself who, manipulating
this new state-controlled medium against an often hostile press,
became a veritable star on television.

Of course in these speeches, which mingled with more nar-
rowly ministerial declarations as with funeral orations on Braque
and Le Corbusier, Malraux never abandoned his own familiar
themes. The same is obviously true of his very many representative journeys abroad, which took him to numerous countries
in North and South America, Africa, and Asia. Yet while only
his visit to the Antilles in 1958 and that to the Republic of Mali
in 1961 could be described as purely political missions, his
cultural expeditions were never devoid of political significance.

In the early years, in Latin America and elsewhere, he was
sometimes quite explicitly offering his own past and his own
reputation as a moral guarantee both that his government was
democratic and that its Algerian policy was not blindly colonial-
ist. In the longer term, from the spectacular speech on the
Acropolis in Athens of 1959 onward, he was playing a missionary
role on behalf of France which had political significance far
beyond the intensification of existing cultural relations. While
he was in some sense simply developing his own view of culture
and his own vision of a universalist France, he was at the same
time suggesting not only that the United States and Soviet
Russia were too materialistic and culturally void to maintain the
essential values of Western civilization, but that these could
best be maintained through a new kind of Third World alliance
of the extended Latin countries and such older civilizations as
India, with France acting as catalyst. What he was in effect
doing—without strain or insincerity, though not without some

tactical trimming of his sails—was providing a cultural justification of de Gaulle's foreign policy at world level.

What then of Malraux's "guarantee to the Left" at home, perhaps the aspect of his activity to be most heavily criticized, particularly with regard to censorship in France and the use of torture in Algeria? As it happens, he was one of those who protested less than a month before the *putsch* of 1958 against the seizure of Henri Alleg's revealing book *La Question*. Upon assuming office, he publicly condemned torture and offered to send to Algeria a commission composed of Camus, Mauriac, and Martin du Gard—a proposal which fell through, for quite accidental reasons. The torture continued, as he was to admit in 1959, and in 1960, in Mexico, he was falling back on the idea of its inevitability in a conflict of this kind. At home, political censorship continued with the seizure of several works on Algeria, notably the documentary *La Gangrène* of 1959 and Pierre Leulliette's *Saint Michel et le dragon* of 1961, while there was actual penalization of those actors who signed the "Manifesto of the 121" of 1960. Was not Malraux—who also lashed out resentfully against intellectuals—betraying not only his earlier stated position and his own past, but the very idea of a liberal culture?

In fact, I consider that Malraux's behavior at this stage can readily be defended. It should be appreciated that the new government was in a quite extraordinary predicament. At the outset, the army and *ultra* elements had been seeking to use de Gaulle not only to retain Algeria but to set up a neo-fascist régime in France, while de Gaulle had in some sense been using them to take over power from the "system." Once in power, however, and after some initial hesitation, he decided that Algeria must be allowed its independence. The consequent operation against the army called therefore for a delicate mixture of doubletalk, doublecross, and appeasement—and indeed for the retention of Michel Debré, loyal but known for his tough line on Algeria, as prime minister. In private in 1959, Malraux described the new republic coldly enough as "a provisional consular régime mandated solely to end the war in Algeria," indicated the operation against the army, and made it colorfully clear to me that the prime minister would not constitute an obstacle. If he decided not to "rock the boat"—which after all had a rather mixed crew—it was because of what he saw as the overriding political priority. It should be added that in condemning torture in 1958, to the great irritation of Algiers, he had gone further than any minister of the Fourth Republic. In fact, it was not for nothing that extremists attempted to assassinate him early in 1962.

What does emerge so far is that, for all the apparently symbolical nature of his role, Malraux over this period was necessarily a politician. And the backlash of May 1968 inevitably inscribes even his more immediately cultural activity in a general political perspective. We must therefore look at both his ministerial performance and his guiding conception of culture.

The new ministry represented a regrouping of various government services relating notably to the arts, architecture and the cinema. While the Fourth Republic had left reasonably solid foundations as regards aid to the drama, the advent of a minister of Malraux's reputation and drive certainly provided a fresh impulse. In the field of restoration, the most obvious improvement was the cleaning of public buildings in Paris, which returned a rather gray city center to its original ochre. But Versailles, the Louvre, and other historic places were also restored, various important measures of protection taken, and a most valuable long-term inventory of national monuments and artistic treasures set in train. In his own favorite area of the plastic arts, Malraux sought not only to bridge the age-old gap between the state and its artists by commissioning work from Braque, Chagall, and André Masson, but to make France a home for world art by organizing a number of spectacular exhibitions. He also increased the number of exhibition halls and set up a new National Center for Contemporary Art.

In certain other areas, his performance was less happy. While this was largely due to objective factors—the smallness of his budget, political opposition, or resistance to change on the part of established institutions such as the Comédie Française— it was also due in part to his own temperament. If in *Le Monde*'s thorough and rather sober survey of his ten years as minister Jean Lacouture described him as "an intermittent symbol," it is because he was better at producing the spectacular idea than at following it through.[2] It is true that he was frequently called abroad, and had a serious illness, but he did not find it easy to delegate responsibility, so that some of his collaborators thought him aloof and rather high-handed. Through a combination of these varied reasons his ambitious plans for the national theaters came to very little, while his relations with the cinema were never particularly good—though he did take steps in 1959 to help the industry through a difficult period. In the long-neglected field of music, on the other hand, he handsomely retrieved certain misjudgments through a reform of musical training and the creation of a new Paris orchestra.

The cornerstone for Malraux himself, of course, was to be the setting up of Maisons de la Culture: multipurpose art centers designed not only to extend Paris standards to the provinces but to foster the interpenetration of the arts by combining facilities for drama, music, film shows, and exhibitions. Although budgetary restrictions prevented the realization of the twenty-one centers originally envisaged, a number of these are already in operation. While in some cases an existing enterprise has simply been renamed—as with the Théâtre de l'Est on the edge of Paris— entirely new complexes have also been created, as at Bourges, Amiens, and Grenoble. The financing of these Maisons, through an equal partnership between the state and the local authority, itself led to some strain, since Malraux rather courageously appointed their directors without regard to political affiliation. The result was that experimentalist left-wing directors often saw themselves as fighting against the local politicians as well as against cultural provincialism. Even so, impressive results were obtained. At least until the crisis of May 1968, when these Maisons de la Culture—several of which were simply to be closed down—appeared to supporters of the regime to have turned into hotbeds of radical contestation.

Yet this irony simply points to the larger contradiction inherent in Malraux's position. I have already suggested that his later "tragic humanism"—with its anti-intellectualist bias, its view that this is the first civilization to have no "meaning for man," and that we are on the way to "reinventing our gods" —is so romantically negative as to be abstract and intellectually rather thin. The cruel fact is that, by continuing as minister to pose the problem of culture in these exalted and starkly fundamentalist terms, he was in some sense evading the issue.

The theoretical approach which followed from this was in fact a limited and a defensive one. Still tied to the perspective of his own art writings, he saw a spiritually empty civilization of science reeling toward disaster unless its "arts of satiation"— the sagas of sex and violence produced by its new "dream factories"—could be balanced by the constant resuscitation of the great arts of the past. Whence a resolutely democratic but apolitical and, in sociological terms, acultural view of culture as a kind of vertical confrontation of the individual with the cosmos outside educational and other structures—and his statement to the National Assembly in October 1966 that the Maison de la Culture was becoming the "religionless cathedral" in which each citizen might have the chance of meeting "what was best in himself." It was this general approach, rather than the practical limitations of his ministerial position, which led him to define the problem of cultural democracy without reference to the whole educational apparatus through which culture is transmitted, as to the new medium of television through which culture—of whatever kind—is increasingly disseminated. At the conceptual level, he had indeed left himself with little more than what Lacouture calls "a sort of egalitarian and nationalist aestheticism."[3]

In the particular context of the Fifth Republic, his pronouncements on culture were bound at moments to seem not only high-pitched, but paternalist and rather marginal. And while he was certainly right in some measure to see the outburst of May 1968 as relating to a general "crisis of civilization," the immediate context of the students' revolt set his own conception of cultural democracy very tellingly in perspective. They were protesting against a system of higher education which was inefficient in practice and undemocratic in scope. They were also protesting against the tone of the regime, as symbolized by a monolithic and mediocre state-controlled television service which did not entertain plurality of opinion. It is particularly unfortunate for Malraux that his own ill-judged and abrupt dismissal of the head of the French Cinémathèque should have led to that "Langlois affair" of February 1968—and television viewers abroad raised an eyebrow at brutal police charges against distinguished film directors in the street—which emerges in retrospect as the dress rehearsal for the revolt which was shortly to rock the regime. In fact, it is bitterly ironical that an earnest conception of cultural democracy should have run into angry, frustrated cries for "participation."

For all that, it must be recognized that both "culture" and "participation" raise problems which complex, advanced societies in general have yet to resolve. Malraux's enterprise was an honorable attempt which at least serves as a valuable term of reference. Again, concrete and often striking results were in fact obtained. Indeed, one can say with some conviction that no other minister for cultural affairs—in this political situation and in the face of the varying difficulties with which he had to contend—could have achieved as much as Malraux achieved. And it is pleasant to think that his name is likely to remain associated with those Maisons de la Culture to which he generously, and with some political courage, devoted a part of his life.

CHAPTER 10

The "Antimemorialist"

O NE obviously cannot conclude a study of Malraux without glancing at what he himself sees as his own probable "conclusion": his ambitiously conceived, as yet incomplete "anti-memoirs."

The bulky *Antimémoires* itself appeared in 1967. Presented by Jean Grosjean on the cover as a "dialogue with destiny" to invite comparison with Aeschylus, Shakespeare, and the Book of Job, it was the publishing event of the year in France and was on the whole warmly received. Malraux had projected further volumes and is in fact, at the moment of writing, working on the second. The original intention was that these would appear only posthumously. However, the death of de Gaulle led him to develop an account of their final meeting at Colombey for separate publication in 1971 under the title *Les Chênes qu'on abat.* . . . I shall deal briefly with this short book in its turn.

I Antimémoires

At one level, *Antimémoires* is an immensely cultivated travel-ogue which follows the course of a journey across the world which Malraux undertook on medical advice in 1965 after his serious illness. Thus the preface is headed "off the coast of Crete," and we move slowly to Egypt, India, and then China, before returning to Paris at the end of the book. Malraux's formidably sharp eye for detail is balanced by his passionate and informed interest in the past of these countries. The im-mediate description of places is excellent, while his great Roman-tic gift for rendering the sense of the mystery of human life as it expresses itself through different civilizations in time leads him at moments to sustained lyrical developments worthy of a Chateaubriand. He was still in office, of course, and it is therefore appropriate that he should cut back, say, to his meeting with Nehru in 1958 or to his strange encounter with de Gaulle at the end of the war—as he also cuts back to his previous visits to these parts as a young man.

At this level, the work achieves a degree of unity through the parallel closeup portraits of three front-rank political leaders of the time: de Gaulle, Nehru, and Mao Tse-tung. Malraux gives an impressively economical account, if from a limited standpoint, of de Gaulle's return to power in 1958; he is particularly good on the theatrical quality of his reception by the National Assembly. He also provides a deeply interesting study of the man himself: his monastic distance, his tendency to see men in terms of their potential historical contribution, his military sense of honor, and his decisiveness.

The affectionate and often moving portrait of Nehru is prepared by a meditation on religion in India arising out of a visit to its holy places, and sustained by a lengthy account of their conversations at the time of Malraux's visit in 1958. Their discussion about East and West, led very much by Malraux, is still largely in terms of *La Tentation de l'Occident*—which provides this section with its title. If Malraux can now more easily go beyond Spengler, he is still concerned about a Western individualism expressing itself at once in "the crucifix and the atomic reactor," and asking this political leader of "a culture of faith" whether a civilization "can for long base its values on anything other than a religion." That both men should be agnostics, that Malraux should later tell his ambassador that even among believers what was once called the soul seems to be dying all over the planet, and that his preoccupation with the future of culture in the developed countries should be met by a very different preoccupation with famine and illiteracy—as Nehru gently reminds him—gives their encounter much interest.

Yet in a strange way neither figure is quite big enough for Malraux's lofty treatment, with its tendency to short-circuit the flat relativity of things and to move instinctively toward a mythic fusion of great man, great historical moment, and great tradition. The portrait of de Gaulle is still limited, and France itself perhaps too small. India is certainly big enough, but Nehru is a little too pragmatic and "English" to fit Malraux's grid, while there is also constantly in the background the dominant figure of Gandhi. It is with the monolithic and mythical Mao that Malraux's high-keyed approach seems to coincide with a momentous historical reality to pay handsome dividends. On the very real myth of this figure, on the fantastic feat of endurance that was the Long March, on the Chinese revolutionary world view, and on the "loneliness" of Mao on the eve of the cultural revolution, Malraux provides compulsive reading. It should be added that this final section, entitled *La Condition humaine,* is completed by an admirably sober meditation—related to the occasion of the removal to the Panthéon of the ashes of the Resistance martyr Jean Moulin—on the system of degradation of the German concentration camps.

Why is it then that the admirer of Malraux's work, obliged in some sense to judge him by his own high standards, may feel that it is this concluding meditation, in the end, which morally saves the volume—that, for all the richness of the material and the quality of the writing, *Antimémoires* as a whole is oddly disappointing, even a little hollow? The reasons are complex and interrelated.

That one central reason is the rather Romantic and myth-making vision itself—which, as suggested, does not always seem fully to cohere with the material—is negatively but sharply underscored by the fourth of the five sections, entitled *La Voie royale.* Here Malraux imagines that at a party in Singapore he once again meets his character Clappique of *La Condition humaine,* who proceeds to read to him the script of a film he has made about Mayrena, a nineteenth-century myth-making adventurer in Indo China who provided a historical prototype for the invention of the "fantasy-character" Perken of *La Voie royale.* The whole episode is of course conceived as a playful "mystification," which suggests now that Malraux is poking fun at the New Cinema, now that he is exorcising his own early temptations by attempting a kind of comic-strip version of the nineteenth-century imperialist adventurer. However the mystification may seem somewhat self-conscious and self-protective, and the section seems often to descend into what it is satirizing. The stylization never achieves itself clearly; the piece is poorly paced; and the writing seems generally like a self-indulgently

slack, wordy, and flat equivalent of the early Cubist pieces.
It is rather longer than the section on China, it is the only
new imaginative writing in the volume—and the only piece of
writing by Malraux, I have to confess, which I have ever found
tedious. If it is indicative of the sense of strain about the work
overall, it is because it suggests that there is no very profound
reverse to Malraux's heroic medal, that without the privileged
subject his overdramatic world of history and great men can
readily invert itself into rather empty ironic farce.

To some extent, also, this strain is due to the fact that Malraux is perhaps attempting too much. For it is not simply that
he is trying to personalize his historical or political materials,
to integrate them into a larger and more intimate set of references
and correspondences, to subordinate them to the themes governing his work as a whole—four of the five sections are named
after his own works. It is not for nothing that he reproduces
the Altenburg colloquy and the scene of the tank attack from
Les Noyers de l'Altenburg, or that there should be symbolical
reference to trees throughout. He is in fact making a belated
attempt—but with mainly recent, nonfictional and not always
entirely suitable elements—at his never completed fictional
summa: *La Lutte avec l'ange.*

It is the complex organization dictated by so ambitious an
enterprise which leads him to shuttle backward and forward
in time and in space in a manner which is sometimes confusing, as it leads to linking devices which—given the materials
he is using—may become artificial. It is very largely this which
dictates the *need* to provide the new fiction about Clappique
in order to balance the sections reproduced from *Les Noyers.*
He is in effect trying to apply a fictional aesthetic to a work of
memoirs, and in some sense obliged thereby to treat himself as
a fictional character. And it is partly for this rather curious technical reason, no doubt, that he is led, for example—and for all
the surface irony—to give a rather wildly inflated account of
his trouble-shooting expedition of 1958 to the Antilles.

Yet this somewhat risky overall stylization was perhaps dictated negatively, in the end, by Malraux's basic stance in these
memoirs. What Koestler calls "the dualism of prophet and
poseur" may be due to some uncertainty about his own image
on Malraux's part after a lengthy and often contentious period

as government minister: to some self-consciousness about presenting himself again to his own public.[1] "This is the time,"
he says in his preface—with a sideways glance at Clara, no
doubt—"when my contemporaries are beginning to tell their
little stories." Arguing against the confessional type of memoirs on the familiar ground that they are dependent upon that
"psychology-of-secrets" which he has always rejected, he takes
the line that he is "not much interested" in himself as an individual, but concerned rather with that part of himself which
"responds to the questions which death raises as to the meaning of the world." He is therefore seeking to orchestrate those
moments—whether experienced in political life, literary creation,
or war—when the "fundamental enigma" has presented itself
"like the score of an unknown music." At the same time, in a
more directly personal fashion and with a faintly surprising sort
of romanticism—in that he tends to stress coincidence, or to speak
of the line of life on the hand—he is interested in the way in which
his life seems at times to have prefigured his own destiny.

The stress in this non-private personal work, therefore, is once
again on "Man" rather than on the individual, on "destiny"
rather than on the continuum of living. Starkly typical as it is,
it does not go without some self-protectiveness and it is also
perhaps more appropriate to the projection of pure fiction. The
risk attendant upon such "antimemoirs" is obviously that, in
refusing to write to the self, Malraux may be led to write to
the public self, to the established reputation, and even to the
"legend." It is fair to say—without painful illustration—that this
danger has not altogether been avoided. *Antimémoires* is rich
in many ways, but it is perhaps not here that the greater Malraux is to be found. The irony is that, through being drawn into
writing above the self, he has not quite done himself justice.

II   Les Chênes qu'on abat . . .

Les Chênes qu'on abat . . . takes its title from a reference in
a couplet by Victor Hugo to a multitude of oaks being chopped
down for the funeral pyre of Hercules. This itself is indicative
of the pitch of Malraux's meditation on de Gaulle, built around
his last visit to the general at Colombey on December 11, 1969.
But the scene itself, however real—"the immense black and

white landscape of the snow covering the whole of France"—is also highly symbolical. For this is of course rather more than the "interview" Malraux wrily puts forward in his preface— where he also tells us that, far from being concerned with a "photograph," he "dreamt of a Greco."

At the general artistic level, he is inserting de Gaulle into the world of his *Antimémoires*. As with Nehru, he himself does much of the talking, whether about his meeting with President Kennedy or about his experiences in Russia in the 1930s. The whole broad field of historical and poetic reference of the first volume is again present, down to the symbolism of trees—which suggests interestingly that it is likely to remain unchanged. "Intimacy with de Gaulle," he tells us, "meant talking not about the taboo subject of himself, but about France—in a certain fashion—and about death." But in this carefully composed piece it is Malraux, subtly, who is dictating the tone of the encounter.

At a more personal level, he is seeing both de Gaulle and himself off the political scene. "This is the end of this man's time," he writes, "and of mine." The publication of the fragment was timed to coincide with that of the posthumous fragment of de Gaulle's own memoirs: *L'Effort 1962-*. . . . If this was a furious Parthian shot from a wounded old warrior, Malraux's art covers this unhappy last salvo with a soft saraband. He cannot quite do what he did with his one remaining unbeaten great man of History, Mao. He largely evades political analysis by defining de Gaulle historically in terms of his defiant gesture of 1940, and by ascribing the 1968 "Events" once again to his "crisis of a civilization without faith." But with this fascinating human document he gives their joint defeat a higher dimension.

It is not simply that he gives us the pathos of the retired president playing with wire puzzles for his grandchildren, or going for a walk with his cat. Or even that he brings out the strangely simple thread running through this formidable life: that of a pre-1914 cadet whose pride and coldness came from a certain shyness, who invested the whole of a traditionalist French Catholic sensibility in a military sense of service to the old idea of nation—and followed this star with lonely obstinacy until he became the "Grand Master of the Order of France." Malraux does more than that. He plays the controlling chorus in this almost telepathically contrapuntal dialogue until he has this embittered and stoically scoffing old man, in his "Saint Bernard's cell" of a study looking on to his ancient Merovingian forest, singing an Aeschylean song. Nobody but Malraux could have produced a memorial of this quality. Nobody can supersede him at this level. It was in some sense he—as the general sardonically reminds him—who invented the word "Gaullism." Faithful to the last, amid what he calls "the funeral procession of a world," he has done his best by de Gaulle.

CHAPTER 11

Conclusion

E VEN as a politician, Malraux has been in the forefront of
the French scene for many years now. As a writer—from
the moment his first novel *Les Conquérants* was banned in Soviet
Russia as in Fascist Italy, and commented upon by Trotsky—
he has occupied a central place in French literary culture for
a startlingly long time. These two careers in combination,
cemented into something approaching myth by the legend of
the man of action and by the controversy surrounding his
development, have made him a spectacular figure among the
important writers of this century.

Yet there is a sense in which this very prominence may operate to his disadvantage. While in some critics it leads to undue
respect and submissiveness, it may lead others abusively to
diminish the writer by attacking the legend or the public figure.
Again, while I have been concerned to bring out the essential
unity underlying Malraux's many-faceted and apparently fluctuating career, the unity itself may be so presented as in the longer
term to do his literary reputation a disservice. The first error of
emphasis, I think, is to present Malraux in terms of an exemplary
life, of which the works are to be seen as the direct illustration.
The opposite error, no doubt, is to present him as the philosopher-
prophet of a new and noble "tragic humanism," of which the
works are to be seen as the measured expression. While it is
entirely understandable that Malraux should be presented in
one or the other fashion during his own lifetime, I think it
unlikely that posterity will judge by such criteria.

At the outset, I suggested that the real adventure of this
spectacular latter-day Romantic has been a strangely intense
confrontation with reality through the mind which makes the
"legend of the man of action" itself look like engaging tinsel.
The older view of Malraux as the "witness" sending back reports

151

on his activity from some embattled front is not only super-
ficial, but damaging—there have been many such "witnesses"
in this century, and their names are already largely forgotten.
The intensity and the pathos of *La Condition humaine*, for example, derive less from the Shanghai of 1927 than from the
artistically controlled projection of a haunting contradiction
of very European extraction. The legend itself is little more than
the surface reflection of the profounder myth-making faculty
of a quite deliberate artist who has always known that his "realistic" fiction is in fact a "rectification of reality" in the service
of an obsessional, imperializing private vision. And just as
Malraux's public career has in practice depended upon his
renown as a novelist, so his reputation in the future is likely to
depend on those qualities which make him—to use his own expression—a "dominated writer."

To say this, of course, is also to imply that Malraux's final
importance, highly intelligent though he is, is not that of the
formal thinker. Here again, the success of *Les Conquérants*
or of *La Condition humaine* is the effect not of intellectual control, but of organic or artistic control over philosophical dis-
order. In any event, as I have already suggested, Malraux's
"tragic humanism" is a rather romantic and hollow conception
which led him, as minister of the Fifth Republic, to operate
in terms of a somewhat inadequate idea of culture. To insist
that "man is the only animal to know that it must die," or that
"ours is the first civilization in history to have no meaning for
man": these are propositions which, at the strict intellectual
level, do not take us very far. They express, and appeal to, a
certain conditioning of the sensibility.

In the end, like the almost eerily outmoded private battle with
Spengler underlying the art writings, they derive from an anguish
in some sense arrested in the intellectual terms of the early
1920s. And the originality of the founding essay which crystallized this anguish, *La Tentation de l'Occident*, lies much less
in its derivative views and shaky philosophical analysis than
in the *tone* of its statement of a new moral distress in the face
of paralysis. There are several respects, as in his nostalgia for a
religious order, or in his vague and rather facile disparagement
of "science" or "knowledge"—which often suggests simply an
attack on French nineteenth-century positivist values as they

had destroyed a Catholic society—in which Malraux seems to have remained something of a prisoner of the troubled cultural situation of the aftermath of World War I. It is here, indeed, that we find the surprising continuity of this apparently fluctuating man of action. Just as the force of his novels springs less from *reportage* than from the obsession of the "dominated writer," so his basic thinking derives less from the lessons of action than from an early "culture-trauma"—itself the projection of an original, self-protective stance defiantly elected in the early 1920s.

Yet it is precisely, if paradoxically, this which makes it probable that Malraux will continue to be seen not only as a major imaginative writer, but as an important term of reference in the history of French thought in the first half of the twentieth century.

The major writer does not so much give "answers" as project the "questions" in such a way as to bring out the final mystery of the human situation. The weakness of the "novelist of ideas" is that his works tend to die along with the ideas themselves. The strength of Malraux as an imaginative writer is that—in accordance with his own coherent and objectively quite important aesthetic of fiction—he is essentially a novelist who enacts the extreme situation in which the "ideas" of the character come sharply up against an ultimate ontological mystery. And what gives his best fiction its peculiar intensity and poignancy is less the dramatic historical moment itself, whether it be a turning point of the Chinese revolution or of the Spanish Civil War, than the coincidence of this with a boundary situation at the metaphysical level. It is in this perspective that I have attempted not only to emphasize the qualities of *L'Espoir*, which I consider to have been generally undervalued, but to bring out the quite extraordinary originality of Malraux's exploration of the "New Man" in his novels of the late 1920s.

However, the obsession of the "dominated writer" which gives Malraux's fiction its power—to the extent that several of his novels have achieved a certain classic status in his own lifetime —makes him an important writer in another respect. For the major writer, as he himself has argued, is one who creates over-all a coherent and compelling world of his own which, in that it has in some sense absorbed the real world, can offer a kind of total challenge to the reader. And, indeed, there is a density, a consistency, a rigor about Malraux's whole enterprise as a writer which makes the entire range of his work of relevance to his readers. Through being thus all of a piece as a writer, he emerges as a major and challenging "figure."

And it is as such, rather than as a formal thinker, that he is likely to have a place in the history of ideas in France. For it is not simply because he gave currency to the vocabulary of the Absurd that he crystallized the malaise of the 1920s, anticipated the tidal wave of French Existentialism, influenced such writers as Sartre and Camus, and, indeed, helped to mold the sensibility of several generations. It is because he transmuted the influences of Nietzsche and Spengler and Dostoevsky into a new and original fusion in terms of his own "private drama," because he projected this drama with great singleness of purpose in the field of the imagination, because he invested symbolical situations and characters with a historical immediacy, a reality, and a mystery which challenged more profoundly than mere ideas. In brief, it is because he played an important part in *creating* the problems of his generation by bodying out a compelling myth.

"The only way in which the mind can escape the absurd," he wrote in "N'était-ce donc que cela?," his essay on T. E. Lawrence, "is to give it form and expression by involving the whole world in it." This—with determination, talent, and a certain moving will to humanity—Malraux has done. In doing so, he has contrived challengingly to confront several generations of readers with some of the major moral and metaphysical choices of his time.

Notes and References

Except in the case of minor items not included in the Selected Bibliography, no references are given to Malraux's own writings.

Observations by Malraux quoted in the text, unless the source has been otherwise indicated, have been made in conversation with the author.

Chapter One

1. André Gide, *Journal (A): 1889-1939* (Paris, 1939), p. 912; Maurice Sachs, *Au Temps du bœuf sur le toit* (Paris, 1937), pp. 203-4.
2. For books by Clara Malraux, see Bibliography.
3. Review of *Défense de l'Occident*, by Henri Massis, *La Nouvelle Revue Française* (Paris, June, 1927), p. 818.
4. Interview with André Laguerre, "Man's Quest," *Time* (New York, July 18, 1955), p. 26.
5. Maurice Chavardès, "André Malraux ou l'Ange casqué," in *Écrivains dans le siècle* (Paris, *Résurrection*, 4e série nos. 14-15, 1947), pp. 205-21.
6. Marginal note no. 25 to Gaëtan Picon, *Malraux par lui-même* (Paris, 1953), p. 66.
7. Emmanuel Mounier, "André Malraux, ou l'impossible déchéance," *Esprit* (Paris, October, 1948), p. 479. Also in *L'Espoir des désespérés* (Paris, 1953), by same author.
8. Speech in Paris of Oct. 23, 1934, "L'Attitude de l'artiste," *Commune* (Paris, Nov., 1934), p. 168. Malraux was reporting here on the 1st Congress of Soviet Writers in Moscow.
9. Claude Mauriac, *Malraux, ou le mal du héros* (Paris, 1946), p. 56.
10. Gaëtan Picon, *op. cit.*, p. 45.
11. Denis Boak, *André Malraux* (London, 1968), pp. 2-3.
12. Interview with Jean Farran, "La Grande Aventure d'André Malraux," *Paris-Match* (Paris, June 19-26, 1954), p. 36.
13. Clara Malraux, *Portrait de Grisélidis* (Paris, 1945), p. 36.
14. Interview with Jean Farran, *loc. cit.*, p. 54.
15. Clara Malraux, *op. cit.*, p. 246.

Chapter Two

1. Julien Green, *Journal*, I (Paris, 1938), p. 23.

2. Paul Valéry, *Variété*, I (Paris, 1924).

3. Interview with Gabriel d'Aubarède, "Rencontre avec Malraux," *Les Nouvelles Littéraires* (Paris, April 3, 1952), pp. 1, 4; Pierre Varillon et Henri Rambaud, *Enquête sur les maîtres de la jeune littérature* (Paris, 1923).

4. W. M. Frohock, *André Malraux and the Tragic Imagination* (Stanford, 1952), p. 21.

5. Nicola Chiaramonte, "Malraux and the Demons of Action," *Partisan Review* (New York, July, 1948, pp. 776-89; Aug., 1948, pp. 912-23); André Vandegans, *La Jeunesse littéraire d'André Malraux* (Paris, 1964).

6. Claude Roy, *Descriptions critiques* (Paris, 1949), p. 226.

7. Clara Malraux, *Le Bruit de nos pas*, II: *Nos vingt ans* (Paris, 1966), p. 113.

8. *L'Impartial* (Saigon, July 21, 1924), p. 1.

9. Walter G. Langlois, *André Malraux: The Indochina Adventure* (New York, 1966), p. vii.

10. *Recueil Général de Jurisprudence, de Doctrine et de Législation coloniales et maritimes*, Année 1925, vol. XXXIV (Paris, 1925), p. 204.

11. *Le Courrier Saïgonnais* (Saigon, June 22, 1925), p. 1.

12. *Saïgon-Républicain* (Saigon, July 11, 1925), p. 1.

13. Paul Morand, "Ces Romanciers où nous mènent-ils?," *Les Nouvelles Littéraires* (Paris, Nov. 10, 1928), p. 1; Clara Malraux, *Le Bruit de nos pas*, III: *Les Combats et les jeux* (Paris, 1969), p. 208.

14. Whereas Clara Malraux maintains that neither of them visited mainland China before 1931, Malraux has recently told Pierre Galante that he was in Shanghai "as a tourist" in 1929, and that he will clear up the Chinese aspect once and for all in the next volume of the *Antimémoires*. See Clara Malraux, *Nos vingt ans, op. cit.*, p. 129; Pierre Galante, *Malraux: quel roman que sa vie* (Paris, 1971), p. 70 and p. 75.

15. Jean Prévost, *Les Caractères* (Paris, 1948), p. 106.

16. Pierre Drieu la Rochelle, *Le Jeune Européen* (Paris, 1927); Marcel Arland, "Sur un nouveau mal du siècle," *La Nouvelle Revue Française* (Paris, Feb., 1924), pp. 149-58.

17. Statement, "André Malraux et l'Orient," *Les Nouvelles Littéraires* (Paris, July 31, 1926), p. 2.

Chapter Three

1. Pierre Drieu la Rochelle, "Malraux, l'Homme nouveau," *La Nouvelle Revue Française* (Paris, Dec., 1930), p. 879.
2. Emmanuel Berl, *La Mort de la pensée bourgeoise* (Paris, 1929), p. 187 and pp. 9-10.
3. Emmanuel Berl, *op. cit.*, pp. 179-80.
4. Auguste Bailly, review in *Candide* (Paris, Nov. 6, 1930), p. 4.
5. Leon Trotsky, "La Révolution étranglée," *La Nouvelle Revue Française* (Paris, April, 1931), pp. 488-501.
6. No. 199 in the standard Brunschvicg editions of the *Pensées*.

Chapter Four

1. "*La Condition humaine* d'André Malraux, jugé par les fascistes italiens," *Lu* (Paris, March 9, 1934), p. 14.
2. Emmanuel Berl, "Le Monde de la solitude," *Marianne* (Paris, May 10, 1933), p. 4.
3. Conrad Brandt, *Stalin's Failure in China, 1924-27* (Cambridge, Mass., 1958). I have dealt with this aspect more fully in my edition of *La Condition humaine* (London, 1968).

Chapter Five

1. Édouard Corniglion-Molinier, *L'Intransigeant* (Paris, May 5, 1934), p. 1.
2. Roger Stéphane, *Fin d'une jeunesse* (Paris, 1954), p. 51.
3. A. M. Petitjean, "Les Écrivains combattants d'Espagne à la Mutualité," *La Nouvelle Revue Française* (Paris, March, 1937), pp. 474-75.

Chapter Six

1. Ramon Fernandez, review, *Marianne* (Paris, Jan. 19, 1938), p. 6.
2. Robert Brasillach, review, *L'Action Française* (Paris, Jan. 6, 1938), p. 6.
3. Henry de Montherlant, *L'Equinoxe de septembre* (Paris, 1938), p. 91.
4. René Girard, "L'Homme et le cosmos dans *L'Espoir* et *Les Noyers de l'Altenburg* d'André Malraux," *PMLA* (New York, March, 1953), p. 50.
5. André Gide, *op. cit.*, p. 1292.
6. Roger Stéphane, *L'Observateur* (Paris, Aug. 28, 1952), p. 16.

Chapter Seven

1. "Bergeret" (a *nom de guerre* used in the Resistance), in Bergeret et Grégoire, *Messages personnels* (Bordeaux, 1945), p. 176. There is a *Lettre-Préface* by Malraux himself.

Chapter Eight

1. Bernard Berenson, *Sunset and Twilight* (London, 1964), p. 494.
2. Claude-Edmonde Magny, "Malraux le fascinateur," *Esprit* (Paris, Oct., 1948), p. 525.
3. In a letter to Armand Hoog, quoted by the latter in "Malraux, Möllberg and Frobenius," *Yale French Studies* No. 18 (New Haven, 1957), p. 95.

Chapter Nine

1. Charles de Gaulle, *Mémoires d'Espoir*, I: *Le Renouveau, 1958-1962* (Paris, 1970), p. 285.
2. Jean Lacouture, "Dix Ans de règne sur la Culture," *Le Monde*, Sélection hebdomadaire (Paris, July 24-30, 1969, p. 10; July 31-Aug. 6, 1969, pp. 1, 10). The expression is used as a subtitle in the first of the two articles.
3. Jean Lacouture, *loc. cit.*, art. I, p. 10.

Chapter Ten

1. Arthur Koestler, review, *The Observer* (London, Sept. 22, 1968), p. 30.

Selected Bibliography

Given the number of Malraux's own publications, and the amount of critical attention paid to both his artistic and his political activities, the bibliography is necessarily very selective. Further references may be found in the standard bibliographies, notably Talvart et Place, *Bibliographie des Auteurs modernes de langue française,* tome 13, 1956, and the successive volumes of the MLA's *French VII Bibliography,* covering the period from 1940 to the present. The place of publication is Paris, unless otherwise indicated.

PRIMARY SOURCES
(Fiction marked with asterisk)

1. *Major Publications*

  La Tentation de l'Occident. Grasset, 1926. *The Temptation of the West.* Tr. by Robert Hollander, New York: Vintage, 1961.
°*Les Conquérants.* Grasset, 1928; *version définitive* with author's *Postface,* 1949. *The Conquerors.* Tr. by Winifred S. Whale. New York: Harcourt, Brace, 1929; London: Cape, 1929. With *Postface,* tr. by Jacques Le Clerq, Boston: Beacon Press, 1956; London: Mayflower, 1956.
°*La Voie royale.* Grasset, 1930. *The Royal Way.* Tr. by Stuart Gilbert. New York: Smith and Haas, 1935; London: Methuen, 1935.
°*La Condition humaine.* Gallimard, 1933. Critical ed. by Cecil Jenkins, London: University of London Press, 1968. *Man's Fate.* Tr. by Haakon M. Chevalier. New York: Smith and Haas, 1934. *Storm in Shanghai.* Tr. by Alastair Macdonald. London: Methuen, 1934; reissued as *Man's Estate,* 1948.
°*Le Temps du mépris.* Gallimard, 1935. *Days of Wrath.* Tr. by Haakon M. Chevalier. New York: Random House, 1936; under the title *Days of Contempt,* London: Gollancz, 1936.
°*L'Espoir.* Gallimard, 1937. *Man's Hope.* Tr. by Stuart Gilbert and Alastair Macdonald. New York: Random House, 1938; under the title, *Days of Hope,* London: Routledge, 1938.
°*Les Noyers de l'Altenburg.* Lausanne: Éditions du Haut-Pays, 1943; Gallimard, 1948. *The Walnut Trees of Altenburg.* Tr. by A. W. Fielding. London: Lehmann, 1952; Toronto: Longmans, 1952.

La Psychologie de l'art. 3 vols. Geneva: Skira, 1947-50. *The Psychology of Art.* 3 vols. Tr. by Stuart Gilbert. New York: Pantheon, 1949-51; vols. I and II only, London: Zwemmer, 1949.

Saturne: essai sur Goya. Gallimard, 1950. *Saturn: an Essay on Goya.* Tr. by C. W. Chilton. New York and London: Phaidon, 1957.

Les Voix du silence. Gallimard, 1951. *The Voices of Silence.* Tr. by Stuart Gilbert. New York: Doubleday, 1953; London: Secker and Warburg, 1954. (Revised version of *La Psychologie de l'art.*)

Le Musée imaginaire de la sculpture mondiale. 3 vols. Gallimard, 1952-54.

La Métamorphose des dieux. Gallimard, 1957. *The Metamorphosis of the Gods.* Tr. by Stuart Gilbert. New York: Doubleday, 1960; London: Secker and Warburg, 1960.

Antimémoires. Gallimard, 1967. *Antimemoirs.* Tr. by Terence Kilmartin. New York: Holt, Rinehart and Winston, 1968; London: Hamish Hamilton, 1968.

Le Triangle noir. Gallimard, 1970. (Collection of three previously published short pieces on Laclos, Goya, and Saint-Just.)

Les Chênes qu'on abat.... Gallimard, 1971. (On de Gaulle.)

Oraisons funèbres. Gallimard, 1971. (Collects eight ministerial speeches: funeral orations, commemorative and other pieces.)

2. *Selected Minor Publications*
(restricted to 50 representative items)

* *Lunes en papier.* Galerie Simon, 1921.

"Aspects d'André Gide." *Action,* 3 (March-April, 1922), 17-21.

Editorials and other articles in *L'Indochine* (June 17-Aug. 14, 1925), and in *L'Indochine Enchaînée* (Nov. 4, 1925-Feb. 24, 1926), Saigon. (Over 50 articles ascribable to Malraux, though not all signed.)

"D'une jeunesse européenne." In *Écrits,* Grasset: Cahiers verts No. 70 (1927), 129-53.

* *Royaume farfelu.* Gallimard, 1928.

Review: *Contes, historiettes et fabliaux* and *Dialogue d'un prêtre et d'un moribond,* by the Marquis de Sade. *Nouvelle Revue Française* (June 1928), 853-55.

* "*Les Conquérants,* fragment inédit." *Bifur* No. 4 (Dec. 1929), 5-15.

Interview. *Monde* (Oct. 18, 1930), p. 4.

Interview. *Candide* (Nov. 13, 1930), p. 3.

"Réponse à Trotsky." *Nouvelle Revue Française* (April 1931), 501-7. Follows article by Trotsky on *Les Conquérants,* 488-501. (Tr. of both in Lewis, see Secondary Sources below.)

Preface: *L'Amant de Lady Chatterley*, by D. H. Lawrence. Gallimard, 1932. (Tr. in *Yale French Studies* No. 11, 1953.)

Preface: *Sanctuaire*, by William Faulkner. Gallimard, 1933. (Tr. in *Yale French Studies* No. 10, 1952.)

*"A l'Hôtel des sensations inédites." *Marianne* (Dec. 13, 1933), p. 5. (Chapter excluded from *La Condition humaine*.)

"Trotsky." *Marianne* (April 25, 1934), p. 3.

"A la découverte de la capitale mystérieuse de la reine de Saba." Ten articles. *L'Intransigeant* (May 3-13, 1934).

Speech in Moscow: "L'Art est une conquête." *Commune* (Sept.-Oct. 1934), 68-71. (Tr. in Malraux number of *Yale French Studies* No. 18, see Secondary Sources below.)

Preface: *Indochine S.O.S.*, by Andrée Viollis. Gallimard, 1935.

Speech: "Réponse aux 64." *Commune* (Dec. 1935), 410-16. Reply to "Manifeste des 64 Intellectuels" supporting Mussolini over Abyssinia, in *Le Temps* (Oct. 4, 1935). (Tr. in *Yale French Studies* No. 18, see Secondary Sources below.)

Review: *Les Nouvelles Nourritures*, by André Gide. *Nouvelle Revue Française* (Dec. 1935), 935-37.

Speech in London: "Sur l'héritage culturel." *Commune* (Sept. 1936), 1-9. (Tr. in *Yale French Studies* No. 18, see Secondary Sources below.)

Speech in New York: "Forging Man's Fate in Spain." *The Nation*, 144 (March 27, 1937), p. 351.

Speech in Madrid. *Commune* (Sept. 1937), 41-43.

Speech before the Mouvement de Libération Nationale. *Combat* (Jan. 26, 1945), 1-2.

Interview (Feb. 1945). In Roger Stéphane, *Fin d'une jeunesse*, La Table Ronde, 1954, 40-69.

Interview. *Labyrinthe* (Feb. 15, 1945), 1-2. (Tr. in *Horizon* No. 70, Oct. 1945.)

Esquisse d'une psychologie du cinéma. Gallimard, 1946; also in *Scènes choisies*, 1946, 324-34. (Tr. in S. K. Langer, ed., *Reflections on Art*, Baltimore: Johns Hopkins, 1958.)

"N'était-ce donc que cela?" *Saisons* No. 3 (Hiver 1946-7), 9-24. On T. E. Lawrence. (Tr. in *Hudson Review*, VII, 1956.)

UNESCO speech: "L'Homme et la culture artistique." J.-J. Pauvert, 1947; also in *Les Conférences de l'UNESCO*, Fontaine, 1947, 75-89. (Tr. in *Reflections on Our Age*, ed. Stephen Spender, New York: Columbia, 1949; London: Allen Wingate, 1948.)

The Case for de Gaulle: a dialogue between André Malraux and James Burnham. New York: Random House, 1949.

Speech (extracts): *Extraits du discours prononcé par André Malraux*. Rassemblement du Peuple Français (1951), 2 pages.

Preface: *Tout Vermeer de Delft*. Gallimard, 1952.

Preface: *Qu'une larme dans l'océan*, by Manès Sperber. Calmann-Lévy, 1952.

Preface: *Van Gogh et les peintres d'Anvers chez le Dr Gachet*, by Michel Florisonne. L'Amour de l'Art, 1952.

Interview. *Les Nouvelles Littéraires* (April 30, 1952), 1, 4.

Congress of Cultural Freedom speech: "Ce que nous avons à défendre." *Preuves*, Supplément: "L'Oeuvre du XXe siècle" (May 1952), 21-23. (Tr. in *Confluence*, Sept. 1952.)

Preface: *Essai de stratégie occidentale*, by General Pierre-Élie Jacquot. Gallimard, 1953.

Interview. *L'Express* (Dec. 25, 1954), 10-11.

Du Musée. Éditions Estienne, 1955.

Interview. *L'Express* (Jan. 29, 1955), 8-10. On the resurgence of the Left. (Tr. in *Yale French Studies* No. 15, 1955.)

Speech in Stockholm (extracts): "André Malraux parle de Rembrandt." *L'Express* (April 20, 1956), 18-19.

Ministerial speech to National Assembly. *Journal Officiel, débats parlementaires* (Nov. 17, 1959), 2498-2500. Also *Le Figaro* (Nov. 19, 1959), p. 6.

Preface: *Sumer*, by André Parrot. Gallimard, 1960.

Speech at French Institute, New York. New York: Ambassade de France, Services Culturels, 1962. (Tr. in Blend, see Secondary Sources below.)

Ministerial speech to National Assembly. *Journal Officiel, débats parlementaires* (Oct. 27, 1966), 3974-76.

Interview. *Le Figaro Littéraire* (Oct. 2-8, 1967), 6-9; (Oct. 9-15, 1967), 12-15; (Oct. 23-29, 1967), 12-15.

Radio interview to Europe No. 1 (extracts). *Encounter* (Jan. 1968), 50-1.

Preface: *Poèmes*, by Louise de Vilmorin. Gallimard, 1970.

Preface: *La Querelle de la fidélité*, by Edmond Michelet. Fayard, 1971.

"La Mort, qui n'est pas loin." *Nouvelle Revue Française* (April 1971), 1-42. Unpublished fragment of *Antimémoires*.

Interview, with the late Jean Vilar. *Magazine Littéraire* (July-Aug. 1971), 10-24.

SECONDARY SOURCES
(Restricted to 35 items in volume form)

BLEND, CHARLES D. *André Malraux: Tragic Humanist* (Ohio State

University Press, 1963). Solid, sympathetic study of Malraux's "tragic humanism."

BLUMENTHAL, GERDA. *André Malraux: the Conquest of Dread* (Baltimore: Johns Hopkins Press, 1960). Perceptive, if somewhat lyrical and generalized essay on the saturnine element in the work.

BOAK, DENIS. *André Malraux* (London: Oxford University Press, 1968). Rather hostile general critical study, useful on the ideas background and on the art writings.

BOISDEFFRE, PIERRE DE. *André Malraux* (Éditions Universitaires, 1952; new ed., 1957). Competent short general presentation.

BRINCOURT, ANDRÉ. *André Malraux, ou le temps du silence* (La Table Ronde, 1966). Pamphlet arguing the inadequacy of Malraux's ministerial approach to cultural affairs.

CARDUNER, JEAN. *La Création romanesque chez Malraux* (Nizet, 1968). Close study of fictional techniques, particularly as regards scene construction and character portrayal.

DELHOMME, JEANNE. *Temps et Destin, essai sur André Malraux* (Gallimard, 1955). Penetrating analysis, rather vitiated by existentialist jargon, of the ontological situation of the individual in Malraux's work.

DORENLOT, F. E. *Malraux, ou l'unité de pensée* (Gallimard, 1970). Thematically organized presentation of Malraux's ideas which seeks, by juxtaposing quotations from different periods and areas of the work, to bring out its overall unity.

DUTHUIT, GEORGES. *Le Musée inimaginable* (Corti, 1956). Monumental 3-volume onslaught on Malraux's art writings; interesting and often stimulating, but vehement and sometimes unfair.

Esprit (Oct. 1948): "Interrogation à Malraux." Lengthy section giving a variety of viewpoints on Malraux's Gaullism, including excellent articles by Claude-Edmonde Magny, Emmanuel Mounier, and Roger Stéphane.

FITCH, BRIAN T. *Les Deux Univers romanesques d'André Malraux* (Lettres Modernes, 1964). Short analysis of two modes of presentation of the self in the novels.

FROHOCK, W. M. *André Malraux and the Tragic Imagination* (Stanford: Stanford University Press, 1952). Early and pioneering general study, which made a notable contribution to the biographical aspect.

GAILLARD, POL. *Malraux* (Bordas, 1970). Illustrated short general presentation.

————— (ed.). *Les Critiques de notre temps et Malraux* (Garnier,

1970). Collection of critical excerpts, which usefully reprints significant reviews of some of the works.

GALANTE, PIERRE (avec le concours d'Yves Salgues). *Malraux: quel roman que sa vie* (Plon: *Paris-Match* et Presses de la Cité, 1971). Journalistic biographical study strongly emphasizing Malraux's sentimental life; of little analytical value, but often informative.

GANNON, EDWARD. *The Honor of Being a Man: the World of André Malraux* (Chicago: Loyola University Press, 1957). Solid and interesting investigation of Malraux's work and agnostic humanism from a Jesuit standpoint.

GAULUPEAU, SERGE. *André Malraux et la mort* (Lettres Modernes, 1969). Well-informed short study illustrating the central importance of the theme of death in the work.

GOLDMANN, LUCIEN. *Pour une sociologie du roman* (Gallimard, 1964); largely devoted to Malraux. For all the interest of Goldmann's problematic and structuralist approach, the actual analysis of the fiction is rather disappointing.

HARTMANN, GEOFFREY H. *Malraux* (London: Bowes & Bowes; New York: Hillary House, 1960). Brief introductory survey.

HOFFMANN, JOSEPH. *L'Humanisme de Malraux* (Klincksieck, 1963). No critical criteria external to the work studied, but this stands out as an excellent and impressively thorough explicitation of Malraux's humanism.

HORVATH, VIOLET M. *André Malraux: the Human Adventure* (New York: New York University Press, 1969). Attempts to view Malraux's work in terms of its presentation of "the human adventure" and of the idea of cyclical flux.

JUILLAND, ILEANA. *Dictionnaire des idées dans l'oeuvre d'André Malraux* (The Hague-Paris: Mouton, 1968). Large and systematic glossary of key terms and concepts in the work; strictly for the specialist.

LANGLOIS, WALTER G. *André Malraux: the Indochina Adventure* (New York: Praeger; London: Pall Mall Press, 1966). Valuable and excellently documented account, if a shade uncritical, of this early episode.

LEWIS, R. W. B. (ed.). *Malraux: a Collection of Critical Essays* (Englewood Cliffs, N.J.: Prentice-Hall, 1964). Helpful compilation containing notably the exchange between Trotsky and Malraux about *Les Conquérants*, as well as valuable contributions by Maurice Blanchot, Vincent Brombert, Nicola Chiaramonte, Joseph Frank, Edmund Wilson, and others.

MALRAUX, CLARA. *Portrait de Grisélidis* (Colbert, 1945). Fictionalized account of the Indo Chinese episode.

————. *Par de plus longs chemins* (Stock, 1953). Novel based on a joint archaeological expedition, with a close psychological study—in barely transposed form—of the young Malraux himself.

————. *Le Bruit de nos pas* (unfinished multivolume autobiography), II, *Nos vingt ans* (Grasset, 1966). Interesting account of the early stage of the marriage, their travels, the expedition to Indo China in search of the statuettes, and her return home to muster help.

————. *Le Bruit de nos pas*, III, *Les Combats et les jeux* (Grasset, 1969). Deals with the second phase of the Indo Chinese episode, involving Malraux's co-editorship of the newspaper *L'Indochine*, up to their return to France around the end of 1925.

MAURIAC, CLAUDE. *Malraux, ou le mal du héros* (Grasset, 1946). Suggestive analysis of the themes of eroticism and heroism in the work.

MOSSUZ, JANINE. *André Malraux et le Gaullisme* (Armand Colin, 1970). Thoroughly documented and, while favorable, balanced account of Malraux's postwar political commitment.

PICON, GAËTAN. *Malraux par lui-même* (Éditions du Seuil, 1953). Intelligent general presentation, sounder than the author's previous study of 1945, and of particular interest because of the annotations by Malraux himself.

RIGHTER, WILLIAM. *The Rhetorical Hero: an essay on the Aesthetics of André Malraux* (London: Routledge & Kegan Paul, 1964). Intelligently sympathetic and balanced short study of the art writings.

VANDEGANS, ANDRÉ. *La Jeunesse littéraire d'André Malraux* (Pauvert, 1964). I think he overvalues the early "Cubist" writings, which Malraux himself laughs off, but this is a formidably well-documented and valuable study of Malraux's artistic formation.

WILKINSON, DAVID. *Malraux: an essay in political criticism* (Cambridge, Mass.: Harvard University Press, 1967). Intelligent study, with interesting viewpoints, if biographical unsoundness makes it unsatisfactory on the earlier work.

Yale French Studies (No. 18, Winter 1957): "Passion and the Intellect, or: André Malraux." Whole issue devoted to Malraux. Includes three of his speeches of the 1930s, as well as useful articles by R.-M. Albérès, Blossom Douthat, René Girard, Armand Hoog, Gaëtan Picon, Charles F. Roedig, and others.

Index

(The works of Malraux are listed under his name)

85061

DATE DUE
